The
**Unfair
Advantage→**

The
Unfair
Advantage →

How Startup Success
Starts With You

ASH ALI & HASAN KUBBA

P

PROFILE BOOKS

First published in Great Britain in 2019 by
Profile Books Ltd
29 Cloth Fair
London EC1A 7JQ
www.profilebooks.com

A CIP catalogue record for this book is available from the British Library.

ISBN 978 1 78816 331 6
eISBN 978 1 78283 597 4

Text design by sue@lambledesign.demon.co.uk
Printed and bound in Great Britain by Clays Ltd, Elcograf S.p.A.

Contents

Contents

Introduction

'How does a startup become so successful?'

As the first marketing director of Just Eat UK, and the number 3 hire on the senior management team, I have been asked this question over and over again. After the phenomenal £1.5 billion Initial Public Offering (IPO) of our online food ordering startup in 2014, people would ask:

'Ash, you were there from the beginning. What is the secret?'

My mind would spin in all different directions trying to think of an accurate answer … Was it the idea? The technology? The 'growth hacks'? The team? The timing? Maybe it was just the sheer hard work and hustle that we put in? What *really* led to one of the largest tech startup IPOs the UK had seen in almost a decade?

We were touted as an extraordinary London-based success story (launched originally in Denmark), and we got a lot of attention. However, every answer I gave about the cause of our success felt as if it was missing a crucial piece of the puzzle … and I could never *quite* put my finger on it.

The beginnings of a theory for startup success began to brew in the back of my mind as I moved on from Just Eat and started a few other companies: first founding my own fully bootstrapped (without external funding or investment) startup called Fare Exchange, a private hire taxi platform, then venturing abroad to start Washplus, an on-demand mobile laundry app – the first of its kind in Dubai.

With Fare Exchange, we developed smart software and digital marketing systems that took taxi bookings which were then serviced by local taxi companies. This was in 2010, years before Uber entered the scene. I grew it at blinding speed, from £0 to £25 million in bookings revenue in just three years – with only five full-time staff. My next startup, Washplus, became Dubai's fastest-growing laundry and dry-cleaning startup.

I developed the reputation for being a 'growth hacker', someone who's good at growing a startup really, really fast. Meanwhile, with the hard-earned money I'd made from my own startup ventures and especially the big Just Eat IPO, I also became an angel investor and advisor, putting my own money on the line by investing in startups and mentoring them.

I've recently started a social impact adult education startup, Uhubs, where the goal isn't just profit, rather it's both profit and positive impact on society. At Uhubs we help people upskill and learn directly from experts in an easy and affordable way.

As my work with startups took me all around the world, from Europe to America, the Middle East to Southeast Asia, I kept thinking about the underlying secret to success in starting businesses. I noticed that founders and investors the world over were running into the same issues and asking me the same questions. Everyone I met was working really hard, but some startups were succeeding while others were failing.

The lie of meritocracy

If I have learned anything on my entrepreneurial journey, it is that the media narrative on startup success can be *very* misleading. Around every corner, you're bombarded with endless myths, hero-worship, PR, and hype around successful entrepreneurs who are heralded as living testaments to the power of hard work, meritocracy, and the American Dream. (Yes, even in the UK and in much of the world in general.)

Silicon Valley and the startup world loves to present itself as a progressive, meritocratic place – with those talented and hardworking enough inevitably rising up above the parapet and reaping the rewards for all the blood, sweat and tears they have put in.

Meritocracy means that those who 'merit' it are the ones who achieve it. In other words, those who deserve to get rich, get rich.

The underlying idea is that we can all be like those amazing billionaire entrepreneurs, if only we pulled our socks up. If only we got up at 4am and hustled hard enough. We read articles and watch news segments about their tips and tricks for success, we read books that tell us we can all be like them if we were simply disciplined enough, hardworking enough, and had enough grit and perseverance.

Bullsh*t.

At a time when inequality is at an all-time high, and as someone who's 'made it' and can now be considered very privileged, I want to relieve us of the *collective delusion* that we're living in an actual pure meritocracy.

Because over my two decades in the startup game, I have begun to see distinct patterns emerge as to which startups succeed and which ones fail. And I'm ready to answer that question: 'How does a startup become so successful?'

In this book, Hasan and I want to break down the factors of success in a way that's both eye-opening, brutally honest, yet still ultimately empowering.

Yes, as a society we have made leaps and bounds in becoming more meritocratic and fair, and that's fantastic. As the son of immigrants who grew up poor in the poorest part of Birmingham, I am grateful that we no longer live in the middle ages where you were either a rich lord or a poor peasant.

However, my experience in the startup scene tells me that we still have a long way to go. The reality is that there are still problems, barriers and un-level playing fields too numerous to count.

As an insider who's been on all sides of the table – from poor to privileged, from employee to entrepreneur, startup founder to angel investor, and mentee to mentor – I'm more convinced than ever of the fact that the path to success is not just self-discipline, belief and hard work.

My co-author Hasan and I see it every day – plenty of hardworking, dedicated, passionate startup founders come to pitch to us at our central London office. Unfortunately, we have to turn away almost all of them and point them in a new direction.

Why? Often it's because they don't understand a simple truth. A truth which defies almost every book title or business headline you see today:

Success in the startup world is not simply awarded to the hardest workers. It is awarded to those who develop and use their Unfair Advantages.

By 'unfair advantage' we do *not* mean an unethical or illegal advantage (although we're sure there are many of those). An unfair advantage is a competitive upper hand, and your set of unfair advantages is unique to you. It's more than just a unique selling point, it's a fundamental leg-up over the competition, and sometimes it's not one that is 'earned' or worked for.

Let's take a very simple example from sport. Being tall is a simple and significant unfair advantage in basketball. It doesn't matter how hard a short basketball player works, they have less of a chance of becoming a professional. That doesn't mean, of course, that there has never been a short professional basketball player, it just makes it much less likely, regardless of whether they work hard or not.

Startup businesses are not physical sports, but similar rules apply: if you're privileged, educated, richer, smarter, you're more likely to win. But luckily, that's not the full extent of it, and unfair advantages can be found in a range of ways in anyone's life.

Virtually every person we speak to agrees with this radical new way of looking at successful startups – whether they're a founder, early employee, venture capitalist or angel investor.

This book is unique in that the primary focus is not the idea, the product, or anything else in the business. This book is about you, the founder, the entrepreneur behind the business (whether you've already launched your startup or are still thinking about it). And the simple reason is that it all starts with you. Startups at the early stage have nothing to show and it's the founder or co-founders who set it up for success.

The business idea is important, and we will talk about it, but before the idea comes You. Here's what influential venture capitalist Eileen Burbidge, founding partner and investor at Passion Capital, had to say:

> …when we first meet a company or business seeking investment, we're simply judging the people. Ideally, we want to assess the team, its tech … and any momentum the company has. But since we invest so early, we almost never find all three. Often the only thing we have to gauge is the team – the founders.

Likewise, that's what we look at before investing in a company, and what any investor worth their salt will look at too.

The goal of traction

Now, the fact that we mention investors and venture capitalists (VCs) is not because every founder should be looking to raise money from them. Far from it, some businesses are better bootstrapped without investors, and kept lean (keeping costs and overheads low). But whether or not you need to raise funding in the first place depends on your unfair advantages, and in that sense funding is a useful way to show how your unfair advantages, the things that sell *you*, are present even before you've got a business bank account. It's very rare to raise funding without having any 'momentum' as Eileen Burbidge calls it. Momentum means getting more and more people to buy or use your product. This is also known as 'traction', in the sense that you're starting to make progress in your startup rather than just 'spinning your wheels' getting nowhere, like a car stuck in deep snow.

Whether or not you intend to get investment into your startup, a big question to address is this: *how* do you attain that elusive traction in the first place? After all, most startups fail not because they can't build a product, but because they can't get enough customers and/or users.

I'm often invited to talk about startups and growing a startup. I always like to start with this slide:

> Most startups fail, not
> because they can't build
> a product.
> But because they can't
> get traction.

To get that momentum, growth, and subsequent success in your startup, you need to have strong unfair advantages as your foundation. By knowing, developing and leveraging your unfair advantages, you will work on the right idea, partner with the right co-founders, and develop a strong foundation.

Starting a company from scratch and then growing it is one of the hardest things you can do. But with the right unfair advantages, and the right mindset, you can be in with a shot.

The book

When Hasan and I first spoke about the Unfair Advantage concept on stage, it resonated in a way we weren't expecting. At the end of each talk, we'd have a long line of attendees – founders, aspiring founders, investors – all lining up to ask us to help them find *their* unfair advantages (and in the case of the investors, to help them find the startups with the unfair advantages so that they could invest in them).

That's why we decided to write this book.

I met Hasan at a business dinner in London. He came across as an astute and humble young entrepreneur who was generating a good (and mostly passive) income for himself with his boutique digital marketing agency. While I had a more intuitive inclination to entrepreneurship from a young age, Hasan's journey began with him investing in an online course. He explained how he got into it for the freedom and independence, and he *got it* straight away when I began to talk about my developing theory of unfair advantages. We became friends and he soon started working with me as my investment partner, sitting through hundreds of startup pitches with me when founders were trying to get investment. The insights we were able to glean together developed into our investment thesis and formed part of a tech startup we began working on. Subsequently we've worked together to develop this concept and put together this book.

We have since advised, mentored and consulted with hundreds of founders at the early stages of their startups. We've each presented The Unfair Advantage model in TEDx talks, at top London universities, and Hasan has been flown out to Dubai as a speaker and mentor at a large international startup summit attended by hundreds of startups. We've spoken to corporations looking to maintain their dominance, launch new products or enter new markets by applying lean startup and Unfair Advantage methodologies.

Now we want to share what we know with you. We want to help you find your own unfair advantages to succeed in your startup, whether you already have one or are planning a launch.

After reading this book, you'll walk away with:

1. A strong understanding of what an Unfair Advantage is for both an individual and for a startup.

2. An understanding of how to find and use your own Unfair Advantages to succeed in business.

3. The Startup Quick-Start Guide – to get you going with a really solid foundation on this crazy journey.

In the world of business, the odds are stacked against you. And startups have a habit of failing, sometimes quite spectacularly. You don't want to be one of the 90 per cent that don't make it.

Stack the deck in your favour to succeed.

This book is your roadmap to putting those odds in your favour – to succeed in starting that startup, to raising that funding, to getting that traction and hopefully getting that big exit if that's what you're after. Hasan and I wish we could have had a book like this at the beginning of our entrepreneurial journeys.

It will help you no matter the challenges you may be facing, whether you need to find a co-founder, get your first customer, juggle a full-time job while getting your startup off the ground, get funding, build an MVP (Minimum Viable Product – which we'll explain in Part III), get users, develop your sales, marketing and growth hacking, generate enough cash to extend your 'runway time' to keep your startup afloat, handle competitors, attract mentors and advisors, and more.

This book is our official answer to the questions we get asked about the success we've been fortunate enough to have in startup businesses. We truly believe that you'll find life-changing value in this book, and a radical and brutally honest, yet still inspirational, way of looking at the world of business success.

If you're thinking of starting your entrepreneurial journey, this book is for you. We can relate so strongly to aspiring founders and that feeling of freedom that you crave, as well as the fear that you feel, and which is holding you back.

And if you're already running a startup, but are struggling with some of those early-stage challenges, this book is also for you.

It is your first step to the fast track. With the information you'll gain from the 'Understand' section (Part One) and the practical steps and MILES Framework in the 'Audit' section (Part Two), you will look at success and your own personal *and* circumstantial strengths and weaknesses like never before.

Equipped with those advantages, you'll be confident and ready for Part Three – 'The Startup Quick-start Guide'. You'll be set to take the startup world by storm, and make those dreams a reality.

Let's dive in!

Ash Ali and Hasan Kubba
London, UK

PART ONE

UNDERSTAND

1

Life is unfair

'I am a young, white, educated male ... I got really, really lucky.
And life isn't fair.'

Those are the words of Evan Spiegel, the billionaire founder of photo-messaging app Snapchat. In our research into startup success, we found his story particularly interesting. According to Forbes, Spiegel was the world's youngest self-made billionaire (before Kylie Jenner that is – more on her later). Born in 1990, he reached $1,000,000,000 aged just 24.

'I got really really lucky. And life isn't fair.'

This part of the quote really stood out to us. Was Evan implying that his success was simply luck? He's led a privileged life, and he knows it. To give you an idea of how 'lucky' he was, let's dive deeper into his background.

Evan Spiegel grew up in a multimillion-dollar household in Los Angeles, surrounded by countless fancy cars, ultra-exclusive country clubs, and luxury holidays all over the world at Four Seasons resorts.

His early years were spent at an expensive private school in LA which curiously enough was also attended by Tinder co-founder Sean Rad, plus a host of Hollywood stars such as Kate Hudson, Jack Black, and Gwyneth Paltrow. His parents also reportedly got him and his sisters elite private tutors at a cost of up to $250 an hour.

Evan's parents were powerful lawyers, his father working on high-profile cases such as the BP oil spill in the Gulf of Mexico and actor Charlie Sheen's infamous $100-million-dollar suit against Warner Brothers. His mother held the distinction of being Harvard Law's youngest female graduate.

When Evan finished high school, his father's powerful connections and considerable clout as an alumnus and donor to Stanford University certainly didn't hurt his son's prospects of getting into the ultra-competitive and prestigious Silicon Valley dream school. Evan's family connections also got him introduced to Peter Wendell, a big-time venture capitalist (VC) and one of Forbes's 100 top venture investors in the United States, with investments in hundreds of successful startups and numerous IPOs.

Not a bad connection to have.

Through Wendell, Evan also met titans like Eric Schmidt, former CEO of Google, Chad Hurley, co-founder of YouTube, and Scott Cook, founder of financial software giant Intuit.

Eric Schmidt later said this about Evan: 'He has superb manners, which he says he got from his mother. He credits his father's long legal calls, which he overheard, as giving him perspective on business and structure as a very young man.'

Scott Cook decided to mentor Evan, gifting him with a wealth of business wisdom as he took his first steps into the tech startup world. Later, Cook put his money where his mentorship was and contributed to Snapchat's first round of funding.

Although he started young, Evan had already received over a century's worth of combined wisdom and business lessons by the time Snapchat began to grow. While many twenty-somethings might have been nervous in big meetings with powerful investors, Evan Spiegel famously stared down one VC who was unwilling to adjust his firm's standard investing terms, telling him: 'If you want standard terms, invest in a standard company.' That VC firm went on to invest in Snapchat's third financing round in 2013.

This is what we're looking at when we talk about unfair advantages. These factors all stacked one on top of the other and contributed in powerful ways to Evan's success with Snapchat and to him becoming Forbes's youngest self-made billionaire.

Evan's connection to wealth, influence, and power directly impacted his success. He was able to climb the ladder at such a young age because he had been largely set up to do so. In fact, he didn't climb the ladder, he went up in a rocket ship.

That's not to say we're attributing *all* of Snapchat's success to Evan's privileged upbringing.

Not at all. Plenty of privileged kids amount to absolutely nothing. As with all success stories, there are a wide variety of factors that play a role. For example, Evan was very smart, and Snapchat had a brilliant insight at its core – that people want to communicate with photos that would 'self-destruct', i.e. disappear after a few seconds. This is something that none of the established social media giants, Facebook, Twitter, or Instagram, had even thought of. Evan not only had access to the funding, the contacts, and the mentors, he executed *brilliantly* on a very timely product. He was in the right place, at the right time, with the right idea. He, his co-founders, and his employees worked really hard *and* really smart to make it a success.

The refreshing thing about Evan? He's upfront in acknowledging how many breaks he's enjoyed along the way. Contrary to the 'buckle down', 'burn the midnight oil' and 'hustle your ass off' advice thrown around all too often in the tech world,

Evan says this:

'It's not about working harder. It's about working the system.'

'Working the system' has unethical connotations, like 'gaming the system' or even 'cheating the system'. We don't mean it in that way, we simply mean that it's not about working harder, it's about working *smarter* to succeed.

In a nutshell, that's what this book is all about: *How* to work smarter, and how to work the system in your favour. And crucially, you don't have to grow up privileged like Evan Spiegel to do it.

The fact is that, as Evan recognised, the world is not fair. And it's more unfair for some than others. He was brought up very rich, extremely well-educated, with very successful parents and social connections. But what if you didn't grow up with any of these advantages? Does this mean you are set up to fail?

That might be how it feels sometimes.

Often, you are told that the only answer to a less-than-ideal situation is to work hard. If that doesn't change anything, work harder! But sometimes, when you're being told to work harder when already at full pelt, and with all the other obstacles and difficulties life may throw your way, this feels like adding insult to injury.

And yet, in every corner of the web and within the self-help and business section of every bookshop, you'll hear the same story: 'Hard work is what makes the difference!' 'Hustlers are the ones who make it!' 'When you wanna succeed as badly as you wanna *breathe*, that's when you become successful.'

An entire industry seems to have grown up around this 'hard work worship'. After all, how many business self-help gurus and motivational speakers claim effort as virtually the only answer? (Well, that and possibly their cheesy 'five-step' program to becoming a millionaire.) Once you buy the course or book or video series, what do you get? Outdated tactics and generic regurgitated advice and 'motivation' to hustle hard.

I mean, don't get us wrong … obviously hard work and sacrifice is a factor. Sacrifice is required for success because you *do* have to forego some short-term pleasures for long-term success. That's a given. However, it's simply too reductive to think that if you don't win, it's because you're being outworked.

This oversimplification of *hard work = success* is not only misleading, it can be downright confusing when you don't know *what* to work hard *on*. Remember what Evan Spiegel said: 'It's not about working harder. It's about working the system.' Working *hard* without working *smart* is useless. For example, you can work incredibly hard designing and building a product, but if it's a product that nobody wants, then tough luck, you'll get nowhere despite your long hours and blood, sweat and tears.

> 'I've seen a lot of hard working entrepreneurs fail, and I've come to the conclusion that working hard, while never a bad thing, is not really the magic thing that leads to great inventions or successful outcomes.'
>
> *Caterina Fake, venture capitalist and co-founder of Flickr*

As a very successful serial entrepreneur and venture capitalist, Caterina Fake should know what she's talking about. Her startup Flickr became one of the world's most popular photo-sharing websites and an early pioneer in social networking, which was very quickly bought by Yahoo for around $20 million. The quote above is from an article she wrote for Business Insider with the title: 'Working Hard is Overrated'. She then went on to found, grow and sell another startup, this time to eBay for a reported $80 million.

As Caterina says, promoting hustle as the one and only 'key' reduces all the nuance of success in business to a simplistic one-size-fits-all solution.

In the case of Evan Spiegel, for example, we also need to think about the level of society he was born into, the world-class private education he received, the confidence instilled in him by his environment, the social graces he picked up from his accomplished parents, the connections his father gave him, and all the amazing self-made billionaire mentors he just happened to gain along the way. We haven't even mentioned the unknown impact of genetics on intelligence, creativity, problem-solving and people skills that Evan inherited from his incredibly successful parents. Also, what role did good fortune play in his success? Is it reasonable to suggest he may have received the benefit of a touch of luck along the way? These all played a role in making Evan not only successful, but *phenomenally* successful.

Uh oh. Did we really just say all that? How *dare* we mention genetics, luck and parental endowment all in one paragraph, in a *business* book!

Well, we told you this isn't your typical business self-help book.

Good old Mr Snapchat is not the only person who has noticed that action alone isn't the answer.

Billionaire angel investor, co-founder of LinkedIn and early senior team member of PayPal Reid Hoffman was asked the following question when a guest on the NPR podcast 'How I Built This':

'How much of what you accomplished is because of your hard work and your intelligence, and how much of it is because of the luck and the privileges that you've had?'

Without a breath of hesitation, he answered:

'... the answer is MASSIVELY BOTH, of course'.

'Massively both'. This is from one of the most wealthy, successful people in today's digital world. It seems that the more successful people are, the more willing they are to admit that factors other than simply hard work played into their success.

In case you're still thinking that this book is about how great it is to grow up privileged like Evan Spiegel, we'll show you how an Unfair Advantage can take many forms. To illustrate this, we'd like to take a couple of examples that are closer to home. Let's take a detailed look at a couple of entrepreneurs who transformed their lives.

Us.

2

Our entrepreneurial journeys

Ash: my story

My parents used to ask me: 'Ash, why is it that when everyone's walking one way, you're walking the opposite?' That was me.

I wasn't trying to rebel or be contrarian for the sake of it. I feel like I've always questioned the approach that everyone else took. This used to really annoy my poor parents. In fact, when I was a teenager, they'd always tell me to keep my mouth closed when we were visiting friends or relatives, because I'd question anything and everything, and end up starting some kind of silly debate.

Maybe that's why my life turned out so different to everyone I knew growing up.

Born and raised in Birmingham to Pakistani immigrant parents, I grew up in a very poor, crime-ridden part of the city. And when I say crime-ridden, I really mean it. We had gangs, drug-dealers, and murderers right on our doorstep. I still remember the police cordoning off half our street because there had been a shotgun murder in the house opposite ours.

Where I came from, unlike Evan Spiegel, we were not surrounded by homes worth millions. The only 'wealth' we saw in our area were brand new BMWs driven around by thugs and shady characters, not lawyers and doctors. And not much has changed, because to this day, I see news stories of murders and burglaries in the area where my parents still live.

I went to a deprived inner-city state school. My family was kind and loving, but as you can tell, their lives weren't exactly overflowing with financial opportunity. I was lucky enough to go to a grammar school later, and that's when I got a small glimpse of how the middle classes lived. It's the little things that I remember, like the feeling I got when my classmates talked about the class ski trip they were going on, and which I wasn't going on because my parents couldn't afford it.

Birmingham is primarily an industrial town, and my Dad had a simple job at the local steel factory with a very simple wage. Mum had her hands full trying to keep up with my siblings and me. As is common with immigrant parents, she believed a good education would pave the way for a better life for her children, so that's what she really focused us on. My parents worked hard and sacrificed everything they could so that their children could have a better life.

And how did I repay them? By dropping out of college. Twice. Not in the cool Mark Zuckerberg kind of way, either. I mean sixth-form college, aged just seventeen. Without connections or a clear path, I floundered. While my siblings did quite well in school and gained plenty of qualifications, I was the black sheep of the family who didn't go to university.

I just didn't have the patience for school. Despite the fact that there were no entrepreneurs in my family, no role models or mentors to give me a guiding hand, I still found myself thinking about my own little money-making ventures.

At age thirteen, I started my first job, a paper round. I quickly realised that it was taking too long every morning, so I decided to sub-contract half the deliveries to one of my friends. The two of us could do the same job in less time as we could cover more ground.

A couple of years later I realised I could make good money by selling encyclopaedia CDs to neighbours and friends. These were the days before Wikipedia. I was so pleased with my little business, and my customers were also very happy. I later discovered that these CDs were pirated and it was illegal – but it was good money until I had this realisation! I loved making a bit of money because for me cash represented freedom and possibility. I didn't even spend it. I just enjoyed having it and knowing I could afford stuff if I wanted it.

Fast forward a few years and all my friends were heading off to university and enjoying the rite-of-passage of moving out, being students and partying it up. And there I was, still in my childhood bedroom at my parents' house. I had a retail job at Staples, a big warehouse shop selling office supplies and computers – which I was quite good at.

During this time one of my old school friends and I began working on our own little project, one which would change my life forever.

My friend's parents owned a shoe warehouse, and he approached me because he knew I was always up for ways to make money. We came up with the wild idea of building a website to sell the shoes online. This was 1998. At the time, nobody was doing eCommerce – even Amazon had only just entered the UK and was focused solely on books. We were too young and excited by the internet to believe everyone telling us that nobody would buy stuff online. And thank god we were.

It wasn't a smooth process. Back then, there were no easy ways to set up a website, no easy ways to take payments online. Every single line of code had to be written from scratch by me, in my parents' attic on an ex-display model computer from work that I was able to get on the cheap.

But I became obsessed with making this work. At Staples, we had books about computers and the internet so after work

I'd sit in the aisles reading about building websites. While I couldn't sit still and learn at school, I was suddenly a model student and was learning voraciously.

I spent long days and long nights in the attic, getting this web-based business up and working. This was in the days of dial-up internet, so when I was connected to the internet, my parents' phone line was busy. This meant that no calls could come in or go out. Mum's friends actually started dropping by the house because they could never get through on the phone! I ignored social events, stopped spending time with friends, and faced down problem after problem. All that mattered to me was making that shoe site better. My family all started calling me a hermit as I never went outside anymore. I'd even quit my job at Staples.

In time we actually started getting visitors to our online shoe shop. This blew my mind. Strangers found our site and sent money to us online! We'd then ship out their shoes. It was amazing.

Meanwhile, the dotcom boom was almost at its peak. Headlines were filled with internet startup success stories. It turned out that other businesses across the world were learning what I had accidentally discovered about the internet – you could sell stuff on it. The internet was having its first heyday. On my nineteenth birthday, I even received a card from my siblings which said:

'Future Dotcom Millionaire'

They all had a good laugh. They were teasing me. After all, nobody in my family *really* believed I could make a proper livelihood online, let alone become a millionaire from it. I must have looked like a crazy person – plugging an extension into the telephone jack and running it 30 feet up the stairs and into the attic. Nobody could see a future in my obsession. Everyone expected that one day I would come to my senses and get things figured out. One day I would do the 'right thing'. One day I'd get a traditional job with a traditional career path.

Instead, I propped the 'Dotcom Millionaire' card up in my attic window and kept working. Every time I sat down to work on the website, I would look at that card. My family didn't know it, but they'd provided me with the fire in my belly to keep going. I was really into self-help books at the time and had faith that hard work would get me the success I wanted.

Very soon, we found ourselves nominated for an internet award. We couldn't believe it! How did they even find us? Suddenly, based on the award nomination, I was being courted by multiple companies to go and work for them in London. They all wanted me to come and transform their businesses by leveraging this 'internet' thing because I was one of very few people who happened to have expertise in this budding new field.

So, with a few of my possessions packed into a rucksack, I set off on the train to London. I arrived with no connections, no knowledge of the city, and no place to live. I didn't even know how to use the tube to get around.

I had four different job interviews lined up but was hired on the spot at the first one, with a salary of £30,000. For me at the time, it was more money than I knew what to do with.

There I was, a fresh-faced, teetotal, Muslim Asian teenager with a strong Brummie accent in a big fancy office environment full of adults who had qualifications and degrees in one of the richest parts of the country. What made it worse was the fact that I was so young, and I looked it! In fact, I looked about fifteen. I was often mistaken for a work experience schoolboy, but was in fact managing people who were in their twenties and thirties.

There were people there who were nice, but there were

also some who resented me for jumping ahead of them – a kid who didn't even go to university. I was very suddenly introduced to two new phenomena, office politics and imposter syndrome.

Some people at the office would throw a snarky comment or two my way, or I'd overhear them talking. Not all were playing the office politics game though, and the man who hired me, in particular, really helped me gain confidence in that corporate office environment.

If my detractors in the real world were tricky to navigate, the ones in my head were even worse. With each day that passed, I had to face the same thoughts:

'What am I doing here?'

'I don't belong here.'

'Why didn't I stay in Birmingham?'

'What are my friends and family up to now?'

'I'm missing out on all the fun at university.'

I felt like a fish out of water. I know now that imposter syndrome is incredibly common, but I didn't know that then. I was telling people what to do at work as a teenager, in a big expensive city, not knowing my way around or knowing anyone there. I didn't even know how to do laundry or cook the simplest meal. Up to this point, my mum had done everything for me.

However, I started to get used to life in London and, despite all these initial worries, I was actually beginning to enjoy myself. I was the whizz kid at the agency who really knew his stuff. Yes, maybe I felt a bit out of place, especially when we all went to the pub for after-work drinks and I was there with my glass of coke with a slice of lime. I had a nice disposable income and was having fun with it. I snagged a corner apartment with an amazing view overlooking the docks in Canary Wharf, and went to work.

All my efforts seemed to be paying off handsomely. I rubbed shoulders with every big name in our new industry, revelling in my reputation as the teenage online marketing genius. The world was my oyster, and I enjoyed spending every bit of money that I earned. At the time, I believed all my success was due to my relentless work ethic. I was doing well, helping people in the company understand websites, search engine optimisation, marketing, and all the internet things that nobody knew about at that stage.

For the first time in my life, people understood me. For the first time in my life, I was surrounded by something other than doubt. For the first time in my life, I felt like I was succeeding. I felt like I was unstoppable, riding the wave of this new technology.

I was wrong.

On the 10th of March 2000, the dotcom bubble burst. The Nasdaq index of leading technology shares peaked, then fell off a cliff. According to the *Los Angeles Times*, it wiped out $5 *trillion* dollars in market value for technology companies. Critics who doubted the internet and dismissed it as just a silly trend felt emboldened. And what happens in the US quickly moves across the Atlantic to the UK.

I was made redundant. My illusions that I had 'made it' quickly evaporated, along with the little savings I had. Beaten and confused, I moved back to my parents' house. The 'whizz kid' had to return to his mummy and daddy. It felt like I'd suddenly failed – even though it had nothing to do with me. Why had this happened? How could this happen?

I felt like a complete loser.

I paid attention to who was made redundant and who wasn't, and for some people it seemed to be nothing to do with how good they were at their jobs. It seemed to depend more on their relationships to senior directors, and other office politics.

I realised that certain advantages were at play here, beyond how hard somebody worked or how good they were at their jobs.

Then, I had an epiphany, and said to myself:

Actually, the reason I got this job in the first place wasn't just that I was good at it, it was because I had got coverage by the internet awards nomination. I would never have even thought of applying for a job in London had they not reached out to me themselves. Part of why I had this job was just dumb luck.

Then I realised it went even deeper than that. I was so lucky to have stumbled into having this highly in-demand skillset at just the right time, precisely as the internet was taking off. If I'd got a job at a clothes shop like some of my other friends, I wouldn't have learned all about computers and the internet through my job.

And if I hadn't had a friend whose parents owned a shoe business, I would never have started our ecommerce venture. Had I not had access to books on computers and the internet, I would never have learnt how to do websites, and how to do online marketing. I learned all these things at just the right time.

If I had listened to what my parents wanted, and gone to university, I probably wouldn't have stumbled into this. Also, if my parents hadn't allowed me to stay at home and engage their phone line on the internet, again, I wouldn't be where I am.

I had so much to be grateful for beyond my own hard work and merits.

And so it dawned on me: the skillset I'd built, my expertise, was my own powerful Unfair Advantage. It allowed me to become a freelance consultant in various companies all over England for a while. Quite quickly, life became even better than what I'd experienced in London. In fact, I soon got an even better job in London, a city which I'd grown to love. And I met and married a wonderful woman, and we now had a child.

I had stability, comfort, and a great salary. However, I felt as if I had hit a ceiling as an employee, even though I was quite senior by this point. I still remember the managing director telling me that they literally could not give me a fourth pay rise as I was already earning more than anybody else in my department. Also, more importantly, I was getting bored.

In the meantime, I had continued to be entrepreneurial in my spare time with various little 'side hustles' (businesses you run in your spare time while in full-time employment). It was fun to build up a little web-based business, then sell it on for a big profit. Sometimes it was very profitable, sometimes it failed, but either way it was really fun to execute on an idea and see how well I could grow it. Yet I was looking for more.

The answer to my yearning came not long after the birth of my daughter. Enter Jesper Buch, leading co-founder of a small Danish startup that was making waves in its small home market. Jesper now wanted to take on international expansion, and to use London as a base. 'I need a marketing director, and I think you're kick ass.' He had heard good things about my ability to think outside the box and produce real results.

I wasn't sure. Online takeaway ordering? I'd be only the third senior member of staff at Just Eat UK, with a very modest salary, but a piece of the pie of the startup (shares) was on offer. I knew only too well that such a piece of the pie is only worth something if the startup succeeds. And I knew how rarely big ambitious startups managed not to fail.

At this stage everyone had their reservations, including my wife.

Although it looks good from where I'm standing now, the choice to leave my comfortable job for a risky startup was anything but a no-brainer back then. I still remember the look on my colleagues' faces when management announced I would be leaving to go to an 'online takeaway website'. What was that look in their eyes? Confusion? Pity? It certainly wasn't jealousy, as most people thought this idea was silly.

Remember, this was 2007. The *very first* iPhone would come out that year. Hardly anyone was actually using the slow internet on their phones, and few could imagine a world where you would need websites on the go. This was before there was such a thing as an app store or mobile apps. Critics and consumers alike would debate whether or not smartphones would even take hold in the market. So we were relying on people ordering food on their home desktop computers and laptops for now – nowhere near as convenient as in today's on-demand smartphone world.

The odds were stacked against us. People ordered takeaways by using their landline phones to make calls, and that's how they'd always done it. But my job had become a gilded cage for too long. It was time for me to jump back into the startup ring.

It was time to take a shot.

Cut to me assembling furniture by hand with David Buttress (the CEO) and Rune Risom (COO) for our new Edgware office. Just three of us, with Jesper travelling back and forth between Denmark, London, and later Holland.

It took very long hours and a lot of hard work.

I was unafraid of getting my hands dirty, selling in the field, doing customer support, trying different marketing tactics.

Finally, in 2009, we raised £10.5 million of Series A

investment funding from VC firm Index Ventures, and I headed up our first TV advert which was scheduled to go out during *X Factor*. We won awards for the ad. It was a very exciting time.

I moved on from Just Eat after three years there, and just a few years after that we had the IPO, floating shares on the London Stock Exchange. I still remember that we originally hoped for £300 million, then revised that to £600 million. When we actually got a valuation in the public markets for £1.5 billion it was *insane*. An amazing moment that gave me true financial freedom overnight. I remember thinking back to that nineteenth birthday card and its words 'Dotcom Millionaire' and I smiled. I called up my sister and we had a good laugh.

Between me leaving and the shares going public, I founded Fare Exchange, and after having the unfair advantage of Money, I was able to become an angel investor as well. I now feel I have sat at all sides of the table, and I have since founded and sold a startup internationally (Washplus in Dubai), and recently founded a social impact EdTech (Education Technology) startup called Uhubs.

Looking back, I'm hugely grateful for all my apparent advantages and disadvantages. All the stuff I've lucked into, and the people who've helped me along the way. Those are the elements that have made me who I am today.

Hasan: my story

You know how some people are clearly 'natural' or 'born' entrepreneurs? Ash, for example.

Well, I'm not. I consider myself an unnatural entrepreneur. I had to learn to develop my instinct for working without an externally imposed structure, without a boss, and as an introvert I had to really push myself to learn to sell, I had to learn to put myself out there, and I had to learn to live with the uncertainty that entrepreneurship creates.

What I mean by unnatural entrepreneur is that I don't fit the mould of someone who's always been starting businesses and thinking of money-making schemes from a young age. Gary Vaynerchuk, social media personality and founder of Vayner-Media, for example, loves to talk about how he was making thousands selling baseball cards when he was a kid. Ash was selling pirated encyclopedia CDs. I never felt inclined to make money as a child or a teen (and if I had, it would have probably been with Pokemon cards rather than baseball cards).

Rather than having some vision and moving towards a set goal from a young age, my journey began with me trying to choose a career path. Like many people I've spoken to, I found that the careers service in my sixth form and university really didn't help much. So, as a smart kid with good grades and an affinity for science, the natural expectation, especially for immigrant parents, is a respectable and prestigious professional career. For Iraqi families, the upper echelons are always: doctor or engineer.

Back in Baghdad, where I was born, my parents got me a 'doctor' cake for my first birthday. They were sure, it seems, that their child would grow up to study medicine.

We moved to England when I was three. I grew up in London and went to the local state school which had a poor academic record. We didn't grow up wealthy – we were eligible for free school meals and income support.

We lived a simple life, especially in those early years, but fortunately for me it was a life filled with stability and love. I did well in school – my parents encouraged academic ability and took me to the library often as a child (I loved to read). Fortunately, as I got older, my parents started to do better financially and were able to afford a private school with a modest fee.

I was on my way to becoming a doctor and fulfilling my parents' dreams. However, this serene bubble burst one day when I suddenly dropped out of university only six months into my first year, because I had decided I didn't want to be a doctor.

Drama ensued. My parents were stunned. How could I suddenly decide it wasn't for me? The biggest problem was, I didn't even know what I wanted to be. All I knew was that I wanted to learn about the world, and not have a life of nurses, patients and hospitals.

I had no notion of wanting to be an entrepreneur. If you'd asked me, I'd have thought you were mad. An entrepreneur? Me?

Like Ash, I didn't grow up with any entrepreneurs in the family. I didn't even know anyone who even spoke about it as if it were a real career path.

After graduating from a good university with an Economics degree, I was still stuck. The typical path from economics, if you're interested in making good money, is to become a banker. But I didn't want to do that either.

Now that I was a graduate the pressure was on. After you finish university, you're supposed to get a job. That's what society teaches. But I hadn't lined up any prospects because I still had no idea what path I wanted to take.

I'd been frugal with my student maintenance loan, and was living at home so wasn't under any financial pressure, but I was feeling the societal and parental pressure. One day, I came across an advert online about learning to start your own online business. It was unique because it wasn't marketed as a way to get filthy rich, but rather as an innovative way to use new technologies to free up more time, make good money by genuinely creating value, and allow you to escape the corporate grind.

Ding ding ding! Sounded like what I was looking for.

It was expensive for a new graduate without a job: a few thousand dollars. But it was an investment. I had seen the course before, and had been too afraid to take it, in case it was a scam, or just wasn't for me. However, this second time around I decided to go for it. I wanted to get to a point where I could live off the money that my online startup would make, with very little effort. I wanted passive income. Finally, I had a goal, and knew what I wanted to do.

I bit the bullet and enrolled. It felt like a big risk. However, luckily, the online course was good and what was taught made a lot of sense. And it wasn't a scam, thank god.

We were encouraged to set our goals and work at our new startups every day.

I was raring to go, fully determined to make my dream a reality. Then suddenly, I wasn't. A few months later, even though I'd made *some* progress planning my first website for my new web design and marketing startup, I was too afraid to launch. What if it wasn't good? What would prospective customers think? My fear and perfectionism got the better of me, even if I couldn't admit that to myself.

So, instead, I got a job. I hadn't given up hope, I just reasoned that a job in sales would teach me the skills necessary to get my business off the ground – because a business is not a business until you get your first customer.

The job was for a small investment brokerage firm. There, rather than the clichéd depictions of posh guys in the City, it was full of working-class East and South London boys who hadn't gone to university, but who had the gift of the gab to be investment brokers. That was their Unfair Advantage.

Every day, I'd watch as they placed call after call to investors. Persuasion was the name of the game, and most of the investors they were calling didn't even know them. In a few minutes, they'd try to get their attention, build rapport, and then attempt to persuade them to invest their hard-earned money with them.

The crazy part was that these investors often did! I couldn't believe it. To get these kinds of results, the social and emotional intelligence of the brokers was off the charts. There was one guy in particular, the top broker, who could expertly read people, understand what they were saying, know when to press in versus lay off, and basically smell whenever a deal needed to be closed.

I only did it for a couple of months but I learned a lot very quickly.

After that I got another job, also sales and also in the City, but one which in many ways felt like the exact opposite of the first one. It was at a large corporate firm that had an established reputation and only hired graduates. I learned the more consultative sales approach here.

Sales is a fantastic way to get started if you want to start your own business, because the skills you learn, and in particular the resilience to the rejection and the 'no's that you develop, are absolutely indispensable.

Armed with these powerful lessons, I quit my day job. A fire had been lit in my belly. I was frustrated with myself over how hard I had worked at these jobs for a boss, and at the fact that I hadn't been able to replicate (at least initially) this focus and hard work for my own business, where I had no one to answer to but myself.

I gave myself one month to land my first client and get my first sale.

This time was different – not just because I had new skills but also because I got myself an 'accountability partner'. This is somebody who's also starting out their entrepreneurial journey. You are there to support each other, act as sounding boards for each other, and push each other outside your comfort zones to build your business. My accountability partner was building a (now very successful) video marketing agency.

With someone to hold me accountable, and a new determination, I got my first client at the end of that first month. It was only £600, but seeing that money go into my bank account was magical.

I had also had a few rejections before then, one of whom got back to me a few months later. He was somebody I was introduced to through a family friend, and he became one of my biggest clients and also a mentor. He was a successful multimillionaire entrepreneur with a traditional business whom I learned so much from. It wasn't easy to land him as a client, but persistence, charm and an eagerness to add value and prove my abilities won through.

My accountability partner started getting sales as well, and we both developed together. It was a magical time, both of us scared as hell but pushing each other to go for it, working from a Starbucks overlooking Wembley Stadium.

However, I realised early on that making websites for clients was not going to get me to my ultimate goal of monthly passive income. And so I started working on a recurring revenue product: Search Engine Optimisation (which just means getting people higher up on Google). It was really tough. I met a lot of cowboys in an unregulated market – supposed SEO experts who promised a lot but rarely delivered. It was a trial by fire but, finally, just when I was going to lose a large client, I nailed it. I learned how to do it myself, again taking online courses and continuously learning. I had developed the ability to spot and hire real talent.

It took me two years to 'growth scrap' my way to a viable startup that was generating real and significant profit (more about 'growth scrapping' in Part Three).

The startup had become my salvation. Never would I end up in a job I hated, working for some boss and counting off the minutes till lunch.

I knew I'd reached the pinnacle when I woke up one morning and realised there was only one task on my to-do list:

1. Invoice your clients

My clients were happy because they were getting the results they wanted, and I was happy because I had set up a system where my team, who were based all over the world, were producing those results very efficiently.

My dream had come true. I was able to travel and explore the world, meeting other people like me who had startups generating income for them while they travelled.

I had finally started living the passive income lifestyle. I genuinely did no work while travelling for weeks on end. My two years of blood, sweat and tears had paid off.

'I earned this', I said to myself as I lay on a beach in Indonesia. I was very pleased with myself. So many people had warned me that what I was pursuing was a total scam, that I'd wasted my money on that online course. So many people had told me that passive income was just a pipe dream. I had proved them wrong, and it felt amazing.

Until a little thing happened that stopped me from feeling so self-satisfied.

One day in 2015, I was in Manila, the capital of the Philippines, and I was on my way to meet another digital nomad, a nineteen-year-old German kid who was making five-figure sums a month doing online marketing. I had escaped London's dreary weather, and was really enjoying the unbelievable friendliness and good cheer of the Filipino people.

As I walked out of my Airbnb, I saw some Filipino children who were standing around in the street. They looked scruffy and were barefoot. They can't have been older than nine or ten years old.

As I walked past I realised they were begging. This was unusual. Not that Manila doesn't have impoverished children, but that it was happening here, in the poshest part of Manila, right in the centre of the business district. I'd already been there a several days and hadn't seen anyone begging in this area before.

I'm used to growing up in a cosmopolitan city with a few beggars here and there, and knowing that we have a welfare system, food banks and safety nets to stop them from literally starving to death. However, here in the Philippines, one of the little girls pointed to the almost-empty bottle of Evian in my hands. She literally just wanted a drink of water.

That absolutely broke my heart.

I handed it over and immediately emptied my pockets for any cash that I had. The look of genuine happiness on their faces, and the sad state that they were in really had an effect on me. It was so upsetting to see a poor little girl literally thirsty for a drink of water.

That's when it hit me, how lucky I was. I understood my unfair advantages. It wasn't just me working hard and making it happen. So much of my success was because I had been set up for it.

My parents had moved to London from Baghdad in 1991, just before Iraq started to get even worse from economic sanctions, which led to widespread malnutrition and hyper-inflation. That child could have been me. Who knows what might have happened to my life had my parents not left when they did.

I had the education, the security, the stability of being a native speaker of English. Also I had the money to invest in my education, to take an online course, to be able to live at home in an expensive city for the year it took me to get my startup off the ground. I had the family and friend connections to get my foot in the door of my first couple of clients. I had the emotional intelligence and communication and persuasion skills to get them to hire my new agency.

Being British and having that passport allowed me to travel the world, and gave me the freedom to be a digital nomad in the first place.

Later that year, I happened to sit next to Ash at a business dinner in London. We became friends. From him, I learned about hyper-growth tech startups, and the Silicon Valley world of VCs, angels, and growth hacking. Ash had recently had the Just Eat IPO and wanted to invest it, and so I became Ash's investment partner for startups.

As we screened startup pitches together, and discussed what made some stand out from others, we developed an idea that has slowly grown. Together, we built a boutique startup training and consultancy business based on the Unfair Advantage concept to help startup founders. We were both aware of our own privileges which enabled us to found successful startups. We've since been invited to speak all over the world. At first, I was nervous about public speaking and training others, but we began getting brilliant feedback, and invitations came from further and further afield.

I've now spoken at many events, in the UK and internationally, with my knowledge and expertise in strategy, digital marketing and fundraising. My path has not been one based on innate brilliance or certainty: I've had failures and false starts, and have had to contend with my own self-discipline. But I have watched others with a keen eye, taken every chance to educate myself, observed and analysed the landscape of startups, and learned from anyone and everyone who has crossed my path. That has been my Unfair Advantage.

3

Success is both hard work and luck

'Work like hell.' Elon Musk
'Luck enters into everybody's life.' Warren Buffett

When it comes to financial success and wealth, there tend to be two leading narratives or mindsets as to how it comes about:
Either we believe that:

▶ Rich people got rich through hard work. Rich people deserve their riches. They *earned* their financial success (meritocracy).

Or that:

▶ Rich people got rich through random events outside their control. It's all about luck, timing, natural talent and fate. Their financial success is *unearned* (fatalism).

You can think of these mindsets as opposite ends of a spectrum. The reality, of course, is firmly in the middle. However, it is useful to consider the extremes to understand our underlying thoughts and beliefs about where financial success comes from.

So far, we have addressed the first narrative: the myth of meritocracy – that hard work and ability alone are what lead to success. But as we saw with Evan Spiegel's story, and even his own analysis of where his success came from, he attributes a lot of it to luck.

It is worth taking a moment to unpack this idea, the luck side of things. If we don't really understand it, we might be tempted to complain and moan about not having certain unfair advantages or we may wonder why some other people have been endowed with so many. We might throw our hands up and say that if it's all down to the luck of the draw, then we may as well not bother.

You have read how both hard work and luck played vital roles in both of our entrepreneurial journeys. We both worked extremely hard, but at the same time we also got very lucky. We were both brought up in stable, loving families in a wealthy developed country with excellent education systems, a free national health service, and with some safety nets to take risks, as we weren't exactly going to end up starving on the streets or anything. We were fortunate enough to be able to live with our parents rent free as we developed our first businesses and were lucky enough not to have serious health issues in our families which would have forced us to be caregivers, and fortunate to be well enough ourselves to pursue these business opportunities. Ash was lucky to be born in the UK, and Hasan was lucky to grow up in London, rather than in the war-torn country of his birth.

Beyond those foundations that we are endlessly grateful for, there are also many moments of serendipity and luck that have helped us on our journeys. Ash luckily got a job in an office supply store selling computers, and books about computers, just as the internet was taking off. Hasan was fortunate to have the money to invest in an online business course, and a network of family and friends in London through which he got his first clients.

So luck doesn't have to be the type of privilege that Evan

Spiegel had. In fact it's equally possible that you have the odds stacked really badly against you, and still come out a success. A prime example of luck, though her story may not seem lucky at all, is Oprah Winfrey.

Luck and talent at work

Oprah Winfrey's is an inspiring rags-to-riches tale. A black girl raised by her grandmother in 1950s rural Mississippi who was traumatised by sexual abuse from a young age, she went on to become North America's first black multibillionaire, and is often ranked the most influential woman in the world.

Oprah grew up so poor that as a child she often wore potato sacks instead of dresses, and she recounts watching her grandmother boil clothes to get them clean. Her childhood was a revolving series of caregivers, and the only consistent thing about her environment was that she was constantly uprooted to go and live with someone else. Passed from her grandmother, to her mother, then her father, and back again, Oprah could scarcely have had a worse childhood.

Aside from the poverty and instability, Oprah also had to overcome a slew of emotional issues. Her younger sister, who had lighter skin, was her mother's favourite. Her mother was a housemaid to rich white families and would make Oprah sleep out on the porch while she and Oprah's baby sister slept inside. To make matters worse, Oprah began to be sexually molested at the age of nine. This incident signalled the beginning of a pattern which would continue at least until her early teens when she gave birth to a premature baby – who died after only two weeks.

You may be familiar with some pieces of her tragic childhood, and unless you have been living under a rock, you are also aware of her larger-than-life success.

So the question is, with such clear disadvantages, how did she rise up to such prominence and success?

What exactly took a young African American girl with such tragic early-life disadvantages and turned her into one of the most influential people on the planet, one whom it is claimed single-handedly turned a million votes in favour of Barack Obama in the 2008 election?

When examining success, you are not going to find just one single cause. What stands out in Oprah's case, however, is a gift that she was born with. Oprah was a child genius.

By the age of just three, Oprah had already been taught to read the Bible by her grandmother who took her to church regularly. There she was nicknamed 'The Preacher' for her uncanny ability to flawlessly recite Bible verses to the congregation.

Little by little, unconsciously at first, Oprah was picking up the very skills that would allow her to captivate audiences decades later. In time, her grandmother and later her father would take her to speak in front of crowds at every church within driving distance. Congregations clamoured to hear this wonder child who spoke like a leader.

'From the time I was eight years old, I was a champion speaker', she says. 'I spoke for every woman's group, every banquet, every church function.'

At school, she was allowed to jump years ahead due to her prodigious reading skills. Her father took her to the library regularly which she absolutely relished, and she took sanctuary from the harshness and trauma of her life in her books.

Long hours at the library, book reports, sermons and speeches to hundreds of people honing her public speaking talent – these are experiences which most children never get, or never have the talent or inclination to make the most of.

Oprah did all this consistently before she turned ten. She

got her 10,000 hours of practice very quickly.

Oprah's stellar trajectory continued. She won a full scholarship to Tennessee State University by winning a public speaking contest. She picked up a radio show aged seventeen – on a full salary. She eventually received a nationally syndicated television show.

But where did all of this start? Hard work and hours put in practising, yes. But also, pure luck that she was born with such phenomenal abilities and a strong inclination to develop them, plus caregivers and teachers who encouraged her natural talents to blossom.

Even being starved of attention by her mother had made her seek approval and attention from public audiences, whether at church, on her radio show, or subsequently on her TV shows.

Not everyone is born with the charisma and communication skills that Oprah possessed. Not everyone has a grandmother who diligently teaches them to read from infancy, or a father who regularly takes them to the library or drives them around to put them in front of audiences to speak and build on their talent. And not everyone who has those opportunities is inclined to relish them like Oprah.

On top of her literacy and oratory skills, one of the secrets to the success of Oprah's daytime TV shows is the empathy, compassion and emotion she brings to them, which her traumatic childhood probably helped her develop. Her own turbulent childhood enabled her to convert that first-hand experience into heartfelt compassion and powerful emotional intelligence. This is an example of an important concept that's at the heart of this book: every disadvantage can have a corresponding advantage, and vice versa. Your circumstances and unfair advantages, whether apparently positive or negative, can be double-edged swords.

Oprah's life has been documented well enough that we can see the connection: without the natural talent she was born with, she wouldn't be where she is today. That combination of innate talent and the parental nurturing of that talent is outside of our control, and therefore part of the randomness and luck of life.

We use Oprah's example because it also clarifies what we mean by luck – it's not always 'lucky', as in positive. Oprah had difficult experiences that were as inseparable from her life as the good ones, and both combine to make her who she is today. That is luck. Equally, luck alone was not enough – it's what she did with it, the way she chose to take those chance elements of her life and make them central to her ambition and practice.

Another notable example of the luck of natural talent is Tiger Woods. Tiger's gift for golf was recognised very early by his father, as Tiger could swing a golf club before he could even walk! At the age of two, Tiger appeared on television putting golf balls and being hailed as a prodigy, and at age three, he shot a score of 48 for nine holes, a respectable score for many adults. Sure enough, his natural talents and his father's nurturing of that talent led to a phenomenal career.

There has recently been a big surge in self-help books and videos which say that talent doesn't exist, that it's somehow *all* about hard work, practice, and putting in the '10,000 hours'.

Bullsh*t.

We give these examples to show that natural, innate talent absolutely does exist. With the ultra-successful, it is usually the foundation from which they build their skill and turn them into a superpower through the 10,000 hours of practice.

Warren Buffett, one of the wealthiest people in the world and the most successful investor in history, credits his success to a lot of luck and innate talent: 'I've had a lot of luck. Just being born in the United States in the 1930s ... I didn't have anything to do with picking the United States! And having decent genes for certain things ... In my case I was sort of wired for capital allocation.'

So the location and timing of his birth, and his natural talent for capital allocation (investment) is what he determines to be the major causes of his success, factors which were totally out of his control. He goes on: 'Just in my own case, I was born in 1930 with two sisters that have every bit the intelligence and drive, but didn't have the same opportunities ... If I'd been black, my future would have been entirely different. If I'd been female, my future would have been entirely different.'

So, he's also lucky to be born the right colour and gender to benefit as well.

Did Warren work hard? Did he get his 10,000 hours? Absolutely he did.

And hard work also plays a very important role because it's true that hard work beats talent when talent doesn't work hard. But combine the two and that's when you get rocket fuel.

We can go even deeper and ask: *why* did Warren work so hard? The answer is he did so because he had a natural affinity for investing. In other words, he *loved* it. Part of being 'wired' for something, or having a talent for something, can be thought of to include the inclination to take part in it, and to practice it and become obsessed with it. They absolutely loved it, they were drawn to it, and so they did it. This is what people mean when they say you've got to find your passion. That's how Oprah became who she is, that's how Tiger did it, and that's how Warren did it. And the same can be said for virtually every big success story: Bill Gates, Mark Zuckerberg,

Larry Page and Sergey Brin, and Richard Branson.

That's how these statistical anomalies of mega-success are made, with a very large endowment of luck, and hard work – and usually the hard work is something that comes easily to them because of their natural talent for it, as well as their passion and obsession with it which means that they're happy to put in the hours.

Warren Buffett says: 'I got to do what I love. It doesn't get any luckier than that … I tap dance to work every morning and every day is exciting.'

Contrast this with the fact that 85 per cent of workers worldwide admitted hating their jobs when surveyed anonymously, according to a 2017 Gallup poll. 'Many people in the world hate their job', the report says. In the UK, only a measly 17 per cent of people love their jobs.

So we're not all fortunate enough to love what we do, or to even know what our 'passion' or 'talent' is. The key, as we'll discuss later in the book, is to experiment and focus on what will add value to others. That way, you can find something valuable to do (i.e. something you will be paid for, whether through entrepreneurship or through employment) and find fulfilment in that.

It may feel defeatist or disempowering to think too much about the idea of luck, because it clashes so drastically with the modern belief that our lives are under our own control.

It might also make us feel uneasy because of the idea of fairness. How is it fair for Evan Spiegel to be born with such strong unfair advantages because of his high socio-economic status? Or you might even say, how is it fair that Oprah was born with such a dynamic and valuable gift?

Life isn't fair.

Life is too random and arbitrary to balance out and give

everyone an equal share. We don't all have the same opportunities. We don't all get what's coming to us. That's why we have to make sure we are compassionate to others and ourselves if life doesn't always turn out quite as well as we'd hoped.

This is a concept that often takes people a while to come to terms with, partly because of the prevalence in our culture of the myth of meritocracy – the idea that hard work *alone* will lead to success.

Belief that we live in a meritocracy is dangerous because it imbues value-judgment, a sense of 'deservedness', to people's positions in life. As philosopher Alain de Botton eloquently puts it:

> … in the Middle Ages in England, when you met a poor person, that person would be described as an unfortunate – i.e. somebody not blessed by good fortune. Nowadays, particularly where the belief that they already live in a pure meritocracy is more rampant, in the United States for example, if you meet someone at the bottom of society, they might unkindly be described as a 'loser'.

The similarity between both positions, between the unfortunate and the loser, is that they're seen to *deserve* their state. This is the root cause of a lot of angst and status anxiety in the developed world. We are living in the midst of an epidemic of mental health issues, including depression, anxiety and even suicide. Part of that is the extreme aspirational attitude that we have when looking at the rich and famous in newspapers, magazines and on social media sites such as Instagram. Just as we can't look at photo-shopped and professionally lit and angled photos of models without feeling bad because we feel like failures in comparison, so it is with business and startup celebrities too.

Sure, we can learn a lot from these success stories, but

the pressure of the idea that anyone can be anything if they just try hard enough imbues us all with too much guilt for not achieving what they have. Startup founder stress and burnout are incredibly common and it's important to look after yourself, your physical and mental health. We have to define success for ourselves in a way that's unconstrained by a narrow view of external achievement, in order to be able to find happiness. We'll talk about that more when we discuss your 'Why' in Part Three of the book.

The existence and power of luck is particularly difficult to swallow for people who are used to consuming a lot of self-help and motivational content, who try to just brute-force success through sheer effort (often accompanied by burnout). Self-development and business books are supposed to be about taking control of your life. But what control does anyone have over when they were born, or their childhoods and the quality of their early education?

None.

The key is to use *both* of these ways of looking at the world – that financial success is earned through effort, and that financial success is just dumb luck. So let us strike a balance between believing that hard work pays off and knowing that luck also plays a role.

Think of these two mindsets as tools in your mental toolbox: sometimes you can summon the belief in the power that you have to shape your future, and sometimes you can think about fortune, luck and fate, and be grateful for what you have rather than being disappointed that things don't turn out quite the way you wish.

This second mindset (fate and luck) is also valuable if you want to avoid worshipping the statistical outliers who have had massive success – the Buffetts, Winfreys and Zuckerbergs of the world – and avoid believing that people who haven't done well in life are simply losers who deserve what they got. It helps us to have compassion and to resist arrogance and a smug feeling of superiority when we do have success, and it also helps us to resist having an inferiority complex and experiencing envy when we see people with more than us.

In *Fooled by Randomness*, Nassim Nicholas Taleb writes that 'Mild success can be explainable by skills and labor. Wild success is attributable to [statistical] variance.' (Taleb, being the statistician that he is, calls luck 'variance'.) So we have to bear in mind all the things outside of our control. This is perfectly encapsulated in what has come to be known as The Serenity Prayer:

> 'God grant me the serenity to accept the things I cannot change, the courage to change the things I can and the wisdom to know the difference.'

Written by theologian Reinhold Niebuhr, it eloquently reminds us of the reality of life, and where our attention and focus should lie.

If you're still not fully convinced, let us ask you this question: How many people do you know who have worked really hard their entire lives and yet are still not free of financial worries?

Or, on the flipside, how many people do you know who are in positions of power and success who don't seem to deserve it? There are plenty of incompetent people who have made successes of themselves as well. I'm sure we've all experienced working for a boss who was utterly inept or even did more harm than good to a company.

Remember, there's nothing *wrong* with luck. As a matter of fact, we're quite fond of it. We want you to have it as well (and strangely, there are studies that show that you can do things to increase your luck, which we'll discuss later in the book). If we skate over the obvious coincidences, serendipity and right-place-right-time occasions of life, we give the wrong impression about what it takes to succeed. People unaware of the true power of luck can become bitter, broken men and women, confused as to why they worked all their lives and didn't reach their goals.

Likewise, if you are unaware of the effect of effort and hard work, and the power that you yourself have to improve your life, then, again, you can become bitter and become inflicted with a disempowering victim mindset, where instead of looking at the things you have in your favour, you focus on what you don't have.

The truth is, your success is the combination of an unaccountably large number factors, moments and decisions. The Unfair Advantage framework, along with the MILES Framework (see Chapter 5), will help you figure out what to focus on, and help map out a path for you to take. More importantly, it can help you decide what actions to take next.

We want to teach you how to work smart. We want you to work, from now on, from a position of strength, and from a foundation of your unfair advantages, in your startup, or even in your career.

If you've been on the grind for a long time, trying to make it happen, but still haven't reached where you want to be, you're probably not using your unfair advantages.

If you're looking to take the plunge and start your own business, you can *massively* increase your chances of success by finding and leveraging your unfair advantages.

If you're part of a large organisation and are looking to maintain your dominance, increase your market share, or launch new products and stay relevant, you've also got to understand and leverage your unfair advantages both personally and as part of your organisation's strategy.

In other words, unfair advantages can take many forms and help you at every stage of your career or business path, and knowing about them, developing them, and leveraging them is the most powerful way to work smarter and stack the deck in your favour to succeed.

But what exactly do we mean by the term 'unfair advantage'?

4

Introducing unfair advantages

Imagine two identical applicants for the same job, Sally and Jenna. They have the same experience, the same qualifications, the same everything.

Sally applies for the job the usual way, through an online portal or jobseeker app. She takes time to write a nice cover letter, she's already spent hours and hours on her CV – the formatting, the wording, trying to make it sound great. She then hits the submit button, crosses her fingers, and hopes for the best.

Jenna, on the other hand, doesn't make such an effort. She has a friend who works at the company. Her friend recommends her and hands her CV directly to the boss.

Who do you think has the better chance of landing the job?

The answer probably came to you straight away. Jenna has a better chance because of the connection, a personal recommendation from a friend who works there.

Viewed from afar, that's the simplest form of unfair advantage. Jenna's friend's recommendation boosts her *status* to the boss, giving her a massive leg-up.

Now imagine if David, whose mother just happened to be a senior manager at the same company, came along looking for a job? Then who has the upper hand? What about if we take it a step further – what if David's mother *owned* the company?

Now that's an even stronger unfair advantage.

We all like to think the world doesn't work this way but we all know it does. Although this example is a clear one, it also highlights the way that particular unfair advantages can be abused. Collectively, we should always try to increase the fairness of society, but remember, we will never be able to fully eradicate human biases that lead to unfair advantages like this. Instead, we want to leverage them instead (hopefully ethically!).

Life isn't fair. But if you use the unfairness of life as an excuse to have a victim mindset, to stop yourself from striving to achieve your goals, to make your dreams a reality, then you're only shooting yourself in the foot.

Our aim is not to make you look at the world and despair, or to think that if there are unfair elements at work then it's not worth trying. Instead, we want to equip you with knowledge of the obstacles in your path, and also the possible shortcuts that are in front of you which you may be unaware of. It's like a headwind – if you're cycling straight into the wind, you're going to find it a lot harder than if you have a strong tailwind behind you pushing you forward. If you know about the wind in advance, then you can plan your cycle ride in the most favourable direction. We want to help you pick your direction.

Hard work, grit and perseverance are required, that's a given. However, success also comes from identifying and then leveraging elements which are outside of your immediate, direct control. We call these elements Unfair Advantages.

An Unfair Advantage is a condition, asset or circumstance that puts you in a favourable business position.

And yes, we *all* have unfair advantages.

Your unfair advantages might be where you were born, who you know and what money you have. Equally, your unfair advantages can be your personal interests, your skills, talent or expertise, your lived experience that gives you a unique insight into a problem, or your ability to access a key audience or build your company in a particularly advantageous place.

A couple of properties of unfair advantages are:

▶ Your Unfair Advantages can't easily be copied or bought.

▶ Your set of Unfair Advantages is unique to you.

Evan Spiegel's business savvy and inter-personal skills couldn't easily be copied because he had absorbed at a young age from his parents and mentors what took them decades to learn. Oprah Winfrey's early audiences were unique to her, and while you can buy speaking courses for your children, you cannot ensure weekly audiences of hundreds through cash alone.. And Ash's own timely expertise and unique insights into eCommerce, SEO and online marketing were exclusive to him.

Now, if you already have a startup, you may be thinking, what about for us? What is our Unfair Advantage?

For any early-stage startup, the Unfair Advantage of that startup is the sum of the individual Unfair Advantages of the founders.

Ask yourself: what do I personally have going for me that few other people do? If you have a co-founder, what *personal* advantage does he or she have?

Always partner up with somebody with unfair advantages that balance out yours.

Make no mistake, every successful company starts with a

personal jumping-off point from the founders, be that money, intelligence, expertise, status or connections.

Your Unfair Advantage is your personal economic moat.

An unfair advantage is similar to what Warren Buffett calls an 'economic moat'. As one of the world's richest men and the most successful investor in history, he is often asked how he has such a knack for picking the winning stocks to invest in. His answer? He only invests in businesses with a strong, sustainable *competitive advantage*, and that competitive advantage can be thought of as a moat around the business, defending it from competitors.

I believe Buffett's theory is not just for businesses, but for everyone.

Competitive advantages are to businesses what Unfair Advantages are to individuals and early-stage startups.

Investors and Venture Capitalists (VCs) expect you to be able to articulate what they call 'your personal edge', or your unfair advantage. If you aren't able to do so, you may have a tough time getting the investments you want.

The impact of the founders on an early-stage startup cannot be overstated. That's why you, the founders, are the ones that investors will be interviewing. You decide the direction of your company. You set the culture at the company. That is why we focus so closely on founders, and what you bring to the table from the beginning.

As a company grows and employs more people, and systemises itself as an entity, the impact of the founders diminishes. The business increases its headcount and develops its own systems, policies and standard operating procedures. From there, rather than having unfair advantages, a company now has sustainable competitive advantages (in the traditional business school sense). Now the company has its own brand power, its own institutional advantages of scale, cash flow, a database of customers, suppliers, and partners. As a founder, or director, your job is now to look at what you're missing in a company and bring someone in, or decide to expand your operations, or ask your marketing and PR team to put a new spin on how you pitch your brand. Larger organisations and corporates should remember to treat every new product launch like an agile, iterative startup, and to look at the people in that team as though they were the founders. They should ask: what are their unfair advantages?

In the very beginning, however, it starts with the individual founder or co-founders, and only them.

Your Unfair Advantage is your leverage.

To paraphrase Archimedes' famous saying: *with a place to stand, and a lever long enough, I can move the world.* In other words, by using *leverage*, you can multiply your impact exponentially to achieve your objective.

By leveraging your unfair advantages, you're working smart. As we mentioned, working hard without working smart is useless. When you work hard, you're putting in the long hours and a lot of effort and energy. Working smart, however, is directing and multiplying that effort and those long hours in the right way to make your business succeed. We all have the same 24 hours in a day. What matters is knowing how to spend that time. Knowing and using your unfair advantages gives powerful leverage.

Your Unfair Advantages can build on each other.

Unfair advantages (just like disadvantages) build one on top of another and have a snowballing effect. They don't just add together, they often multiply together. In other words, the more unfair advantages you can stack up in life, and the earlier in life you can develop them, the stronger they will be.

As unfair advantages lead to success through action, there is a positive feedback loop that develops which only increases the success further. Just as with the 'magic of compound interest' which, when started early, leads to massive success over time, similarly unfair advantages and early success lead to stronger unfair advantages, and that success begets more success.

Malcolm Gladwell refers to this kind of virtuous circle in his seminal book, *Outliers*. In it, one of the examples he looks at is that of Canadian hockey players, who are registered in youth leagues aged 9 or 10 based on their birth year. He explains how those born in the earlier months of the year tend to do better because they are older and more developed, so tend to be bigger and stronger than those born in the later months of the year. This leads them to get selected for more coaching and practice, purely based on the luck of which month of the year they were born in. This has been shown to have continued effects and has led to more people born in the first three months of the year becoming professional hockey players. It is also an observed effect in European football players, and American baseball players.

This is referred to as the 'relative age effect' and has been shown to be true in school as well. Studies show that it has long-lasting effects on life outcomes, with those born at the end of the cut-off point for academia, in August, for example, significantly less likely to attend university than those born in September.

Here's how Gladwell sums it up in *Outliers The Story of Success* (emphasis added):

It is those who are successful ... who are most likely to be given the kinds of special opportunities that lead to further success. It's the rich who get the biggest tax breaks. It's the best students who get the best teaching and most attention. And it's the biggest nine- and ten-year-olds who get the most coaching and practice. **Success is the result of what sociologists like to call 'accumulative advantage.'**

Runaway success is what everyone is after. A snowball rolling down a hill gets bigger and bigger at an exponential rate as it gets heavier and larger. As it speeds up, it picks up snow even faster until a fist-sized snowball has become enormous.

Such is the nature of success, and that's why small changes in initial conditions, like winning what Warren Buffett calls the ovarian lottery (the good fortune of being born to the right parents, in the right place, at the right time), and then enjoying other unfair advantages, can make a huge difference to future success.

An always-busy restaurant will attract more diners who want to try it.

A film that's a box-office success will attract more movie-goers.

A book that's a bestseller will attract more sales.

A YouTube video with lots of views will generate more views.

A website ranked high on Google will attract more links from other websites, and therefore will rank even higher.

In this context, the more unfair advantages you have, the more you are likely to accrue. The key is to start identifying and developing your own unfair advantages as soon as possible, no matter your age.

Unfair Advantages give you speed.

Unfair advantages are a *shortcut* to success. They offer you incredible speed. And in startups, speed is the name of the game, as you have to very quickly iterate and test different products, different marketing, different strategies to see how the market responds. You have to learn, pivot, and see what gets traction. Traction is growth, and fast growth is the name of the game.

As Paul Graham, co-founder of Y Combinator, often cited as the most powerful startup incubator in the world, says:

'Startup = Growth. A startup is a company designed to grow fast.'

In a world where market giants and big funded startups can make one decision and crush fifteen budding startups, speed is absolutely critical to survival.

And similarly, if you're an executive at a large dominant company, and you don't want to be overtaken by the innovative little startups that are snapping at your heels, you need that startup speed.

Speed is what finding and leveraging your unfair advantages gives you – it's the rocket ship you and your team need.

Unfair advantages are privileges, or they are built on a foundation of privileges. For example, being born in a wealthy developed country is an unfair advantage, but so is having a particular expertise. Expertise feels like the most meritocratic and 'fair' unfair advantage, but in fact it is built on a foundation of luck, of having the opportunity or baseline education to develop that expertise. That's why we consider the expertise in marketing and growth that we developed in our journeys still to be unfair advantages.

All of what you earn through effort comes from a base of what you've lucked into, whether that's your place of birth, your good fortune to be born in this time in history, the love you've received growing up, the education you've received from childhood, the relationships you developed or grew up with, your health, and even your innate personality including your inclinations and talents.

You can work to develop unfair advantages for yourself, based on what you have to start with – you can get an education, develop expertise, move cities or even countries, make friends and expand your networks, and, most importantly, change your mindset. These are unfair advantages that you can develop proactively.

Unsure what your unfair advantage might be? You are not alone. Believe it or not, most people have *no idea* what their advantages are, and if they have some inkling, it's usually restricted to knowing about their strengths in the form of *skills*. Skills and expertise are important, but there's much more to it than that.

That's why we've developed the MILES Framework – a tool which cuts through the one-size-fits-all approach of the business self-help industry.

PART TWO

AUDIT

5

Introducing the MILES Framework

'Know thyself' Socrates

'Before dreaming about the future or making plans, you have to articulate what you already have going for you – as entrepreneurs do.' These are the words of Reid Hoffman, co-founder of LinkedIn, in his book *The Startup of You*. He and his co-author Ben Casnocha were trying to illustrate how exactly a person could transform themselves by applying startup business principles directly to an individual career. They wrote that line 'as entrepreneurs do' with the assumption that *all* entrepreneurs naturally assess themselves before embarking on any business endeavour.

In our research and first-hand experience mentoring entrepreneurs, however, we've found that entrepreneurs rarely if ever carry out this kind of 'audit', let alone the kind that we are recommending.

It is critical to know yourself because that self-awareness will make your path in life so much clearer. Becoming more in touch with your motivations, personality and mindset allows you to understand and develop your unfair advantages. It also allows you to develop those motivations and mindsets, and even develop new unfair advantages.

Our fundamental idea is that in any field, ultra-successful people (including the much-heralded startup founders) achieve their success through a combination of ability, unique opportunities, and the type of random advantages that come from being born into a particular family and culture that supports their talents.

Until now, there has been no model at an entrepreneur's disposal to help them comprehensively discover and audit their assets, both internal and external, earned and unearned, psychological and circumstantial. This is the exact purpose of our MILES Framework.

The MILES Framework is a powerful tool to help you identify your unfair advantages. It will tell you whether you should be focusing on leveraging your location, whether your education sets you apart, or whether your true strength lies in your status.

The Framework

Unfair Advantages are not just about your strengths, which is what you'll often read about in business and self-help books. The unique thing about the Unfair Advantage concept is that it also takes into account your *circumstances*.

Through our extensive observation of the startup world, and encounters with both successful and unsuccessful founders, we've identified five categories of unfair advantages, which comprise the MILES Framework. Yours will fall into one or more of the following:

Money
Intelligence and Insight
Location and Luck
Education and Expertise
Status

Money is the capital you have, or that you can easily raise.

Intelligence and Insight includes 'book smarts', social and emotional intelligence, as well as creativity.

Location and Luck is all about being in the right place at the right time.

Education and Expertise is both your formal schooling and also your self-learning, which gives you intellectual and technical know-how.

Status is your social status, including your network and connections. It's your 'personal brand' – in other words, how you come across. It also includes your inner status, which is your confidence and self-esteem.

Remember, you don't need to have all of these unfair advantages to succeed. The best strategy is to partner up with co-founders who have unfair advantages that complement yours.

All of these advantages are built on the foundation of *Mindset*, which is the one you have the most control over and where you have the most leverage. You can see this illustrated in the diagram:

The MILES Framework™

The unfair advantage you're likely to have heard about most is money, but it's not the only one. One reason we have worked so hard to develop this tool is to remove the excuse of money. After all, Jan Koum, founder of WhatsApp, has a story that is very different to Evan Spiegel's.

Jan is a tech startup titan now, but didn't exactly start out that way. When he was moving into a house provided by social services, nobody could have predicted he would one day have a net worth of around $10 billion. How did he do it? Not only by 'working hard', but by leveraging his unfair advantages.

In Jan's case, this meant leveraging his incredibly strong expertise as a computer programmer by joining an infamous Silicon Valley hacker club early in his career. On top of that, his strong privacy and anti-advertising ideals, developed from growing up in communist Ukraine, meant that WhatsApp was never designed with advertising in mind, which is part of what made it very popular.

For startups and small businesses, success is not just about MBA frameworks and strategies. It's not about being better, faster and cheaper – those aren't real unfair advantages because they're not sustainable. But when the founding team has a combination of: Money, Intelligence and Insight, Location and Luck, Education and Expertise, and Status, that's when they have a real Unfair Advantage.

It is not enough to know what an unfair advantage is – you need to discover which ones you have. The MILES Framework and the practical sections at the end of each of the upcoming chapters will help with that, but it is also important to start with the questions below, which will help you to determine the basis you are working from before you've even looked at your unfair advantages: your motivation and your personality.

Your motivation – why are you doing what you do?

At the core of your mindset is your 'why'. Why are you striving to achieve what you want to achieve? Why become a startup founder and entrepreneur in the first place?

Simon Sinek has popularised the concept of 'starting with why'. He points out that all companies should first begin by considering why they exist, and then allowing that purpose to flow through everything they do to their customers.

It is very important to have a sense of 'why' as an entrepreneur or founder. At the core of your actions (whether you are aware of it or not) is a deeper belief and sense of purpose guiding the choices you make. Your 'why' can change over time based on the experiences you have, but as human beings, when it comes down to it, we're usually driven by just a few core motivations. As you embark on your startup journey, ask yourself *why* you're doing what you're doing, and *why* you have set yourself such a goal.

Due to the arbitrary and unequal distribution of unfair advantages, your 'why' is particularly important in terms of how you **define success for yourself**. Ideally, your 'why' must come from you alone, because if it is driven by other people's expectations, or a need for approval from others, suffering will be the outcome even if you succeed. Asking yourself that question will help you determine your real motivations for striving to achieve what you want to achieve.

We will talk more about your 'why' in Part Three, when we will consider your internal and external motivations for launching your own startup. For now though, it is enough to think about it and allow your subconscious to ponder the question.

What is your personality type?

Psychologists have devoted decades of research in trying to answer this question. The classification most widely accepted in psychology is that of the 'Big 5' personality traits:

▶ Openness – how open you are to new experiences, and how imaginative you are

▶ Conscientiousness – how organised, self-disciplined and goal oriented you are

▶ Extraversion – how much you enjoy spending your time socially

▶ Agreeableness – how friendly, compassionate and cooperative you are

▶ Neuroticism – how prone you are to worry, anxiety or stress

Where you score in these personality traits determines what actions you need to take as an entrepreneur. For example, Hasan is an introvert so scores low on the trait of Extraversion compared to Ash, but meeting people, expanding your network and building relationships is required in entrepreneurship. He knows he has to be more proactive in meeting and talking to people.

Ash, on the other hand, scores so highly on Openness that he finds it challenging to say 'no' to new opportunities and the new ideas that he constantly has. Limiting the number of projects he works on, and therefore having more focus, has helped him to become a more productive and impactful entrepreneur.

Studies show that there is no one personality type that is ideal for entrepreneurship, however, it is important to have an idea of where you stand so you can act accordingly. The trait that's probably the most *unsuited* to entrepreneurship is high neuroticism. If you're very high on neuroticism, entrepreneurship is not likely to be something you'd enjoy, as it is very stressful and filled with uncertainty. You will need a healthy dose of emotional stability because of the incredibly high highs and low lows in starting and running a business. It may be worth considering doing something with less risk to help manage your mental health.

The number one trait to consider after neuroticism is being visionary, which is very similar to the trait of openness. It's important as an entrepreneur to be curious, to have ideas, and to be unafraid to experience new things. Every other trait has less of an effect, especially if you balance out your weaknesses by partnering up with a co-founder who has the complementary strength. For example, if you are very introverted, it helps to partner with somebody who is more of an extrovert. Likewise for the trait of conscientiousness, if you are not organised (but maybe more visionary and creative), it can help to partner with somebody who is.

Another popular tool to better understand your personality is the Myers-Briggs assessment.

The Myers-Briggs assessment might be the most common personality test in the world. We see it pop up on people's internet bios, résumés, or even business cards.

There are many great free tests online, and also many bad ones. Do your research, avoid the silly ones that you'll see on social media, and focus on a couple of good ones that are backed by research. Consider what they say about you, and how that reflects on your life experiences.

Don't worry too much about the results, especially if you find yourself disagreeing with them. These are just indicators. Many of these tests remain works-in-progress and can change over time, and the results can even depend on how you felt on the day of taking the test. What's important is the self-reflection that taking the test induces. This introspection is very helpful as a way to consider which paths to take to find success, which type of startup, which industry, and even whether you would instead prefer to hedge the risks of launching a startup by being an employee at an early-stage startup, or even doing it as a side hustle while maintaining a day job. It's also important to consult the people who know you, whether they're family, friends, colleagues or roommates. They will give you great insight as well.

Before we get on to the pillars of the MILES Framework, it is critical to address the foundation. Without this foundation, you could stack every unfair advantage in the world and still find yourself unhappy and unsuccessful. That foundation is your Mindset.

6

Mindset

The right mindset is the right place to start with the MILES Framework because it is where you can have the most immediate effect. You can change your mindset in an instant, simply by looking at your circumstances and your life situation through a different lens.

For example, one amazing 'mindset hack' is gratitude. Focusing on what you're grateful for in life can make you feel happier, less stressed and more focused, all without having to change your external circumstances at all. This then allows you to work better and feel better about the work you've done. All of which shows how your mindset can affect both the quality and outcomes of your life.

Another reason we start with mindset is that you can boil down the message in our book to: 'mind over matter, but matter still matters'. In other words, while some self-help books will tell you that you can achieve anything if you set your mind to it, we are more reality based and believe that the physical and biological world has its limits. You're not going to win the Nobel Prize for physics simply by believing in it strongly. But equally, if you don't believe you can do something in the first place, you're unlikely to achieve it.

The Unfair Advantage approach can be misconstrued as being too limiting. Some might claim that our line of thinking is self-defeating. Not at all: having a grasp of the factors of success, including the arbitrary and random ones that are circumstantial and unearned, is not a reason to feel sorry for yourself. On the surface, you can look at the premise we've laid out here and assume that because you don't have money, status, or an education now, you won't be able to gain any leverage in the future.

Nothing could be further from the truth.

Growth Mindset vs Fixed Mindset

According to Dr Carol Dweck, professor of psychology at Stanford University, people with a Fixed Mindset believe they are born naturally gifted at doing some things, but incapable of others. This black-and-white way of thinking often obstructs their development. Failure is a disaster to a person with fixed mindset. When it happens, they will bury their heads in the sand or blame others.

The opposite of this fixed mindset is a Growth Mindset. This is when a person believes that all of life is fluid. Yes, you can be bad at something, but it is only because you have not taken the time or attention to get better at it. The growth mindset is perfectly encapsulated in one word: *yet*. 'I can't write code … *yet*.' 'I can't write a business plan … *yet*.' 'I can't find a co-founder … *yet.*' This three-letter word opens up a whole realm of possibility.

While the growth mindset is by far the better option of the two presented, it still isn't quite the mindset you need to embrace for success.

After all, you can't really say 'I am not a trillionaire … *yet!*', 'I'm not a professional footballer … *yet!*', 'I'm not the first person to travel to Mars … *yet!*'.

Realistically, you simply won't be any of those things. The flaw of the growth mindset idea is that it often ignores the stacks of unfair advantages (and luck) some people already have in life. The first trillionaire is likely to be a tech company titan who is already a billionaire – we'd predict Amazon's Jeff Bezos. The people who will succeed as professional footballers are probably less than 18 years old and have been training to be professional footballers since they were young children. And the first person to travel to Mars is training to be an astronaut right now, or is likely a billionaire again (our money would be on Elon Musk).

We make the most misleading assumptions by looking at outliers, and believing that the only reason we haven't achieved the same is because we simply weren't driven, self-disciplined and hardworking enough.

When reviewing the success of a Mark Zuckerberg, an Oprah Winfrey, an Evan Spiegel, or a Sara Blakely (the billionaire US underwear magnate), we sometimes overlook the unfair advantages in their success which they had no control over.

The ability to think 'the sky is the limit!' is an excellent tool in your mental toolbox. However, there does need to be an element of realism in your thinking, though not one that overly limits you. You need to find the right balance. If you *only* think 'the sky is the limit!' then your head will be full of crazy daydreams, but when you look around at your life and see the huge disparity between your dreams and your current situation, you may experience guilt, disappointment and distress. You'll blame yourself, or you might become bitter and blame everybody else.

All this can be avoided by defining success for yourself in a way that's process oriented, and which focuses on taking action and on enjoying the journey of life. This focus should take into account inner fulfilment, not just quantifiable financial success (which will never be 100 per cent in your control).

Rather than ignore both schools of thought, we'd like to offer a third way of thinking. We call it a **Reality-Growth Mindset**.

A reality-growth mindset is the ability to accept the hard limits of the way things are (the physical laws of the universe) *and* believe that anything is possible (the metaphysical way of looking at the universe). It acknowledges that there are limitations, but that those limitations are more malleable than some people may think.

You have to have these two opposing viewpoints in your mind without feeling the need to fully reconcile them, and then deploy the right perspective when needed. Again, think of them as mental tools in your toolbox.

Sometimes you need to believe that anything is possible to get you inspired and motivated to take action (and sometimes the universe surprises you by giving you more than you even imagined). Other times, it's good to know that you're probably not going to be an extreme outlier, and to enjoy the simpler things in life, because it's true that the best things in life are free.

Reality-growth mindset is the balance between self-awareness and self-belief. Self-awareness says 'I understand I will probably never win a Nobel prize, or cure cancer, or become president or prime minister, or become the world's richest person.' Self-belief says 'I am going to succeed in my own way, and even if my goal feels like a stretch, I can step up to the challenge, and probably have a lot more impact than I can even imagine.'

Reality-growth mindset is about having your feet rooted on the ground, with your head in the clouds. Not just your head in the clouds believing *anything* is possible! And not just your feet on the ground thinking I can never be above average and ordinary. You need both! It is about setting achievable goals rather than looking at outliers and anomalies. You want to be on the cover of *Forbes* or *Time* magazine? Okay, but how about starting with the goal of creating a company that makes profit? One thing at a time, then maybe one day that magazine cover will seem like a reasonable goal.

But remember, we don't *need* to be on the cover of *Forbes*, *Vanity Fair* or *Time*. We don't *need* to be famous to be happy, fulfilled and successful. In fact, it might be more of a hindrance than a help.

There is power in wanting something badly enough. Hasan loves to use the analogy of Harry Potter and the Sorting Hat. If you are nerdy enough to know or remember, in the magical world that J.K. Rowling created, the Sorting Hat is a talking hat which, when you put it on analyses your personality and strengths, and assigns you to one of the houses of Hogwarts. When Harry puts it on, the Sorting Hat wants to put him in Slytherin, the most ambitious and cunning house (and most linked to dark magic and evil), but because Harry so badly doesn't want to be in Slytherin, the hat gives in and puts him in Gryffindor, his dream sorting. This is a great way of saying that if you want something badly enough, it has power to change you.

This power has a limit though, and that's where 'reality'

comes into the reality-growth mindset.

For example, Larry Page and Sergey Brin just so happened to be attending grad school together at Stanford in the mid-1990s when the internet was still in its infancy. During this time, they conceived of and created the prototype for Google, with the help of mentors at the university who encouraged and guided them.

But the internet is no longer in its infancy. And if you never had the grades or the money to get into Stanford, you won't have the same access to a brilliant, skilled and like-minded co-founder. The two had an insight and applied their inspired expertise in a very new industry, and simply executed well. They had a technological unfair advantage based on their expertise which simply created a better product. It would be impossible for you to create Google in the same way today. Even if you did want to build a competing search engine, you would need some kind of unique insight or technological unfair advantage. This is a truth. It doesn't mean success is out of reach for you. It means you will have to take a different path, and leverage your own unique set of unfair advantages.

Unfair advantages exist. Talent exists. Luck exists. Sexism, ageism, nepotism, prejudice, social connections, inherited money, better educations – these are all irrefutable truths. By and large, you are born into an extravaganza of fixed variables that you do not control. You must accept this. At the same time, you *also* must believe you are the master of your own future. You can take responsibility for the outcomes in your life. You can achieve *virtually* anything you set your mind to, as long as what you set your mind to is within the realms of possibility for you, based on your strengths and assets (your unfair advantages).

This precise duality of thinking is necessary. Lean too far towards the unfairness of life, and you become a victim. Lean too far into the 'fully-in-control master and architect of your future' side, and you become disillusioned when your million-aire status doesn't appear after a couple of years of hustle.

Many entrepreneurs didn't have any kind of huge vision when they set up their company. In fact, often it was just a side-project they were working on. Google and Facebook weren't set up as a bid to achieve world domination. But they just grew and grew as their founders realised how good their solution and timing was.

Some entrepreneurs do have that huge vision of course. Jeff Bezos had it in his mind from the beginning to dominate retail, contrary to the myth that he just wanted to do an online bookshop. Oprah always knew she would achieve something huge for herself, and Sara Blakely wrote down that she'd change the world.

Ash didn't think he'd be a dotcom millionaire when he first set up the shoe eCommerce website and started making money. He just enjoyed the ride of making money on the internet.

Hasan had to be convinced by the marketing and sales of an online business course to take the plunge, and he only wanted to make passive income and give himself the freedom to not have a boss.

There isn't a single path to financial freedom and living the life and having the impact you want.

Reality-growth mindset is the fertile soil from which your unfair advantages spring. Treat it properly and you will see a wealth of opportunity pop up all around you. Even though nothing will have changed about your situation, this mindset will show you a whole new world.

Without the right mindset, you can't get very far. After all, there are rich kids with tons of unfair advantages who have amounted to nothing. All the world lay at their feet, yet they never took action. Perhaps an even better example in today's world is the huge numbers of people who have paid huge amounts of money for an education they are not using! Still others have status, but may not be leveraging it. Yes, we start from what we have and what we are born into, but we also start from how we see the world, and what we are driven to do in it – and we can change these things in our favour at any time.

Four characteristics of a strong reality-growth mindset

1. Vision

This is the first irrefutable characteristic of all strong mindsets. You may have heard the expression 'without vision, people perish'. Also without vision, companies lose their way, people lose their jobs, and executives lose their minds.

In a 2017 Forbes review of existing data around character-istics of entrepreneurs, 'vision' rose above 23 others in a list of useful personality traits:

> Vision, interestingly, stood apart from the other four top traits in an important way: Vision was not closely correlated with any other particular traits from the list … vision, therefore, appears to be a more universal, essential trait than any other.

Vision is the ability to see plainly what will exist. It's not magic, it's imagination and goal-setting. While Larry and Sergey, and Mark Zuckerberg didn't have a huge vision at the beginning, they developed it as they went along and saw the potential. Vision doesn't need to be enormous. Huda Kattan, whose story is coming up later, just wanted to do makeup.

That's often all you need to get started. Also it may be all you need in general. The founders of Basecamp, the project management app, are all about having a balanced work and life, and they rightly teach that you don't need world domination to have a great life of success and happiness as an entrepreneur.

People will follow a leader with vision, even if that vision turns out, in the end, to be a poor one. The person with vision serves as a prophet, voicing the unknown and bringing it into reality. If you are not able to imagine the future with your product or service, there is really little reason to continue moving forward. One setback, and you're done.

When you have vision, you can literally see the future you wish to create. As founder and real estate investor Jamal King says:

> I don't mean 'think about things.' Some people just think about things. It's a thought. I'm not talking about thoughts. I'm talking about vision. The visions I have ... are so real. They are so real that when the actual vision comes about, I'm like 'yeah, I've seen this before'.

It sounds like a superpower, doesn't it? But many successful people have noted a similar experience. Oprah Winfrey commented on an event she attended at four years of age, when she dreamt of a different life:

> I remember standing on the back porch ... and my grandmother was boiling clothes ... and poking them down, and I was watching her from the back porch. I was four years old, and I remember thinking 'My life won't be like this. It will be better.' It wasn't from a place of arrogance it was just from a place of knowing that things could be different for me somehow.

Oprah didn't just dream about a different circumstance for herself. She saw it. And then she lived it.

When Ash first joined Just Eat, he would spend hours talking with the management team about how big the company could get. They would sit down for lunch and say things like 'I think this can be a £50 million company and here's why.' The next time, the value would increase to £100 million. Then £150 million. In the early days, the vision got bigger and bigger as they saw more and more potential.

Even Ash and the senior team did not imagine the real figure of the IPO, but vision allowed him and his colleagues to dream in that direction.

2. Resourcefulness

'An entrepreneur is someone who will jump off a cliff and assemble an airplane on the way down.' This is a great quote by Reid Hoffman which perfectly describes the resourcefulness and ability to solve problems quickly that an entrepreneur needs.

Ash has successfully exited a few startups and has started several others which never got off the ground. You may wonder why this is the case. Should there be a better way to plan for these things?

In a word: no.

Certainly an experienced entrepreneur, investor, founder, or early startup employee can take steps to mitigate risk, but the danger can never be truly eliminated. One reason for this is that when you follow the call of an entrepreneur, you probably intend to step into an area where nobody has been before. You will break things. When things break, you will probably see your business in a whole new way.

It's all about having faith in your ability to come up with solutions.

3. Constant growth and lifelong learning

Lifelong learning is probably needed more now than at any

other point in history. Perhaps in years past, you could get a degree and it would serve you for life. This is no longer the case.

The progress curve of technology keeps getting steeper, and acceleration is the result. Entire industries are being upended by startups. We will soon have 5G technology, artificial intelligence and self-driving cars. Even as we write this, business models are changing and new tools and platforms are being created.

Now, some of the biggest and best companies in the world, including Apple, Google, Costco, Whole Foods, and Hilton Hotels, have removed university degrees as a requirement for a job.

From this point on, the future belongs to the person who will commit to a life of constant growth through continuous learning.

4. Grit and perseverance

Each of the case studies we've looked at so far in this book have required a level of grit. In other words, that person kept going in the face of resistance.

Rejections, pitfalls and obstacles will consistently get in your way. Without perseverance, your startup won't make it out alive.

You need thick skin. You need to be able to handle criticism, both the constructive and destructive types of criticism. You have to be able to bounce back even when you're down. Even when you fail. You have to be able to take responsibility, because when you're a founder, there is no one that you can blame.

It's tough. Only grit, doggedness and a very healthy dose of optimism can see you through.

7

Money

'It takes money to make money.'

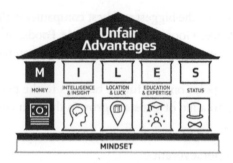

Hasan had a conversation with the ex-head of Search Engine Optimisation (SEO – which basically means getting to the top of search engines) at Zoopla, a UK-based property technology (proptech) startup that also IPO'd in 2014 (and was started at around the same time as Just Eat in the UK).

Like Just Eat, Zoopla had astoundingly fast growth, and SEO was one of their main growth drivers. SEO is a really difficult and time-consuming task. It has an important impact for businesses and an appeal for customers – you get found faster and appear more reputable – and so understandably, every company wants to be at the top of Google.

He revealed the secret to their SEO success. Would you like to know what it was?

Acquisitions.

That's right, they simply *bought out* all the companies whose websites were ranking higher than them on Google. They muscled their way to the top with the funding they had raised, by buying out the other players.

Now isn't that interesting?

When we're talking about money, we mean wealth. Wealth is more than just money, it is also any assets that you own (houses, land, stocks, anything you can sell for money).

Ash especially knows that money matters, because, as you saw in his story, he has experienced what it's like to have it, and what it's like not to have it. It's a completely different world.

Here's one thing in particular that he noticed: rich people often intentionally obscure how easy it is for them to make even more money. And they also know how to pay less than you'd expect in taxes. He finds it strange to talk to other wealthy people and to sense from them this attitude of 'I earned this. I worked for it.' But they forget how much easier it is to make money once you already have it. Rich people own assets, which create more money just by sitting there. For example, if you own a property which you are renting out, you are probably going to be making money every month.

Money is also known as 'capital'. That's why institutional startup investors are called venture capitalists, because they inject capital (money) into a startup.

Money is not the only type of capital we have though. Sociologist Pierre Bourdieu says we all have three forms of capital: economic capital (money), social capital (our network of friends and allies) and cultural capital, which is essentially everything else that can get you respect or prestige (for example, knowledge, qualifications, titles, occupation, how you talk, your accent, how you dress, your body language, your tastes and hobbies, etc.).

Economic capital is what we're referring to in this chapter, with the other two types of capital falling under the 'Status' heading in the MILES Framework.

Having a lot of money is an unfair advantage. Being able to fund your own startup is an unfair advantage. Not having the pressure of living payslip to payslip just to pay the rent and the bills is huge in terms of giving you the time to get your startup profitable (or to get the next round of funding for hyper-growth startups, which often take a long time to become profitable).

Runways and burn rates

In the strange world of startups, the time you have until your startup runs out of money and is forced to close down is called your runway time. You could have four months of runway time, or you could have one year. It depends on how much money you have and how much money you're 'burning'. Your 'burn rate' is how much money your startup is losing every month. If your startup has £5,000 in the bank, and your burn rate is £1,000 a month, then you have five months of runway time.

More money means you have a longer runway. Also, the lower your burn rate, the more runway time you'll have as well.

This is a very useful concept in startups because startup businesses can take anything from a few months to a few years before they become profitable. This is especially true for hyper-growth startups which don't aim to be profitable but rather aim to get as much growth (as many users or customers) as possible, and then eventually start making a profit.

For example, it may surprise many people to know that as of 2019, Uber still wasn't profitable. They've just been burning money at an incredible rate this whole time, and the reason they can do that is because they are able to keep raising more and more money from investors. These investors are patient and confident that eventually the company will become profitable.

But even if you don't have access to virtually endless funding like Uber and are planning to bootstrap a lifestyle startup that is designed to make a profit, you still need to figure out your personal runway time to assess how long you'll be able to live without a salary. This is obviously easier if you're starting out with a large amount of money, but even then, you need to know your runway. Lots of money can become no money if you miscalculate that.

If you haven't yet taken the plunge into working on a startup full time, you can do two things to keep going. One is to cut your costs (reduce your burn rate) and the other is to increase your money. Cutting your costs can mean simplifying your lifestyle (for example, if you're young and single, moving in with your parents, if you're lucky enough to be able to do that, is a tried and true method). And for a startup, staying lean with your spending (being frugal) is always key, as saving money is important to extend your runway time and give you time to make a profit. However, do be careful of being too frugal and not investing in things that your startup needs to succeed.

So, this is how having a lot of money can be a huge unfair advantage. But don't despair – not having a lot of money can also have its benefits. We'll get to that later.

Finally, as we'll discuss in Chapter 17 (Fundraising), the first people to invest in a startup after the founders them-selves are the three Fs: Family, Friends and Fools. Of course, 'fools' is tongue-in-cheek and reflects the high risk of investing in a startup, and hopefully they wouldn't be foolish to invest in yours. However, your ability to raise funding through knowing rich people and being able to convince them to give you investment can also be thought of as a Money advantage. For example, if your friends and family are wealthy, they can afford to take a punt and invest in your startup.

Euan Blair – the bank of Mum and Dad

After an investment banking career, 32-year-old Euan wanted to do something with more social impact. Along with a co-founder, he started WhiteHat, a tech startup company that aims to get more young people into apprenticeships rather than 'useless' university degrees.

However, startups are tough. In its first year WhiteHat had already made a loss of around £400,000. Luckily for Euan and his co-founder, however, they received a capital contribution of almost £600,000 that same year. That capital contribution was completely interest-free.

Phew! Completely saved!

So, where did this money come from?

The source of the contribution was unnamed.

However, Euan Blair didn't have a normal childhood. He grew up in one of the most famous addresses in the world, 10 Downing Street. His father is Tony Blair, former prime minister of the UK.

Tony Blair was nicknamed 'money-bags Blair' in the media for the astronomical sums of money he made after coming out of office (he was reported to be charging up to £250,000 per speech).

The Blairs have declined to comment on whether they gave WhiteHat its 'capital contribution'. But the Blair bank of Mum and Dad had been generous in the past. Euan and his mother Cherie co-own a £4.4 million townhouse in Central London, and also a large property portfolio.

Are we arguing that it was somehow unethical or wrong for the Blairs to help their son in this way?

Not at all. We are arguing, however, that this is a massive unfair advantage. And even if you're not the child of millionaires, having a 'bank of mum and dad' to call upon can give you a huge leg-up.

Since their initial bailout, WhiteHat has gone on to secure at least $20 million of funding according to Crunchbase.

So is money all you need to succeed in startups?

Absolutely not. Nowhere near. So many multimillion-dollar-funded startups have failed spectacularly.

Shyp, founded to make shipping items globally as easy as 'two taps on a smartphone', raised an enormous $62.1 million in investment. It failed and closed down completely in 2018, laying off all its staff.

Beepi, a used car marketplace startup, raised an eye-watering $149 million, but also failed completely.

So money is not the only factor, of course, but is a big unfair advantage. Jan Koum, co-founder of WhatsApp, had $400,000 in savings from working at Yahoo (developer jobs can be very lucrative!). Mark Zuckerberg was able to raise $50,000 from friends and family alone.

Money as a cushion

'Even if I fell I'd land on a bunch of money' – Jay-Z, Album: *American Gangster*, Track: 'Success' ft. Nas.

Jay-Z is referring to money as a financial cushion – if he fell on it, i.e. if he failed in a venture, he'd still be fine. That's the great thing about wealth, it's a safety net in case anything goes wrong. It's a powerful contingency. That's how privileged entrepreneurs can manage risk. They have a big fat safety net of money to fall on.

They're not going to end up on the streets; they're never going to have to worry about their next meal.

However, it doesn't have to be as drastic as becoming homeless and hungry, because if you're really privileged, even your lifestyle doesn't get affected by losing some money in a startup, whereas for your average middle- or working-class person it can be more of a hit.

That's one of the reasons why it's quite common to see rich kids becoming startup founders. Other indirect factors to do with Education and Status also come into play, as we'll discuss in the coming chapters.

Story from Ash:

Recently I did some indoor rock climbing sessions and one of the first things we learned was how to fall properly from various heights, starting at a few inches above the ground to half our height to above our height. Falling properly/failing meant we would be able to get up and do it again. Not learning this could mean a catastrophic event, even death according to the forms we signed off!

In the startup world, nobody teaches you how to fail properly so that you can easily get back up and start again. Some people have the cushion of money, but if you don't have that, then learning how to fail is even more important.

We never get to read 'Seven Secrets of Failure' from the graveyard of failed entrepreneurs, pop stars, actors or writers. We all gravitate towards the 'successful' because we somehow think they have a secret or habit we don't have and that we need.

Usually these very successful people are actually

outliers. If we were to plot them on a scatter diagram it would clearly show how we focus too much on outliers and too little on the reality of those who could really help us achieve success, those who are 5–10 years ahead of us rather than the billionaires.

Money as your unfair advantage

Usually, you know if you've got Money. If you're not sure, go check your bank account now. But of course, you may not be sure if you've got *enough* money for it to count as a true unfair advantage.

A good general rule of thumb is that you need at least 6–1 8 months of runway time if you're going to quit a full-time job and focus on a startup. So to decide whether Money is your particular unfair advantage, ask yourself:

▶ Do I have that capital in my bank accounts now (whether current, savings, or ISAs)?

▶ Do I have friends and family who might invest that money upfront?

▶ Can I save that money doing my current job?

If you have the money to start your business and give yourself the runway you need, great. That means Money is one of your unfair advantages.

If not, what can you do about this? Money can be a factor that's outside of your immediate control. If you don't have rich parents or aunts and uncles, or don't have good credit for instance to get a bank loan, what can you do?

The main thing to consider if you don't have the unfair advantage of Money is to **build a business that doesn't have a high startup cost, and doesn't need to burn much money**

before it becomes profitable. In other words, get paying customers fast. Let that be your first priority. This can be thought of as a 'lifestyle startup'. These are startups that don't need to burn much money, and are profitable much sooner than 'hyper-growth startups', which are Silicon Valley style startups aiming to become worth over a billion dollars. Their strategy to get there is through hyper-growth, without much focus on profitability. There's more information on choosing the type of startup that you want in Part III.

The only exception to this is if you have the ability and credibility to raise funding from just the idea stage. This is quite rare – usually you need good traction and momentum in your startup to be able to raise funding. You have to have a lot of the other unfair advantages in the MILES Framework, ideally a previous successful startup, to be able to pull it off. But it's totally possible.

Here are just a few other suggestions, some of which focus on the most monetisable skills, others which look at ways of increasing your income:

Minimise living expenses We all do this: we buy stuff we don't need. Cut down on this – that stuff probably isn't making you happier and you might be spending all that money to impress people who don't even care about you. By setting yourself a budget, saving money and being thriftier, you can extend your runway times and give yourself more time to become profitable or raise funding.

Learn marketing and sales If you study and apply marketing and sales, you will acquire a skill that is perpetually monetisable – there are always plenty of business owners whom you can help get more customers. You'll be creating value, and will be recompensed accordingly. This is a business idea that is always valid, and is what Hasan did on a small scale, and what

Gary Vaynerchuk is doing on a large scale with his marketing agency VaynerMedia. This is a way to get paying customers fast – you're offering them a service. Even more importantly, you can apply marketing and sales techniques to your own startup to start generating revenue.

Raise funding By learning to pitch and having a good team and idea (a powerful insight into a problem and a strong solution), you can raise funding from investors. This is the least desirable option in some cases because investors often become like your boss, and they take big chunks of your business, but for some people with the right hyper-growth startup idea and the right Expertise and Status, it's a fantastic way to go. Virtually all the big success stories got there through funding. There is more about funding in Part Three.

Learn to code There are plenty of free and affordable books, courses and information on how to code. Not only does knowing how to code mean you can create your own product for your own startup with very little cost, coding is very well-paid, and you can freelance or get a full-time job doing it. This is a great way to make money to build yourself a runway.

Freelance By learning an in-demand skill, whether that be sales and marketing or coding as we already mentioned, or anything like UX design, content writing, or social media management, you'll be able to make money in your spare time to supplement your full-time job or even as a career in and of itself. As you freelance your way to building your capital, your startup will be your side hustle – until one day, you can focus full time on your startup.

Poverty and startup entrepreneurship

If you are living in extreme poverty or financial instability, and if you are living with the stress and fear that comes from not being able to meet bill payments, rent or mortgage, these are *definitely* not the right circumstances in which to embark upon a startup. The same goes for if you have children and dependents that you need to support. You need to have your basic needs met before you can even think about founding a business – that means food and water, a place to sleep, and the feeling of safety.

If you're reading this, you're probably not in poverty. However, it's important to acknowledge that variations of this instability can affect many of us at different points in our lives.

This is the main reason why many intelligent people are now advocating for a Universal Basic Income (UBI) to keep people out of this situation – a situation and mindset of scarcity. It's been proven that living in such scarcity actually lowers your IQ, and makes you act in ways that may be less than beneficial. From Elon Musk and Mark Zuckerberg to Tim Berners-Lee who invented the worldwide web, there are many advocates of UBI. We're also firm believers in it, and see it as a partial solution to the problem we'll face from automation and artificial intelligence. As AI makes more and more jobs redundant, UBI could be a financial cushion for everyone.

Universal Basic Income (UBI) is a possible solution to meeting people's basic needs and freeing them up to be aspirational and creative rather than just desperate. Worrying about crippling debt and where you'll get your next meal is not a great recipe for startup entrepreneurship. US entrepreneur and 2020 Democratic presidential candidate Andrew Yang is another big proponent of UBI and says some very interesting things about it. He proposes giving every American $1000 a month no questions asked, because technology, artificial intelligence and automation are going to kill a lot of jobs that people rely on for a livelihood.

Money as a double-edged sword

As we've mentioned, every unfair advantage has a flipside. Having a lot of money isn't necessarily a good thing, and not having a lot of money isn't necessarily a bad thing.

If you are in less dire straits than extreme poverty, if you're young, fortunate enough to be able to keep living with your parents, don't have any children or people that you're looking after, but are way below where you'd like to be financially, that's a great place to start.

Ash didn't have money, so he was all in. He had the simple safety net of living with his parents, so he had nothing to lose and everything to gain. That made him hungry and ambitious. Hasan had a little bit of runway because he was frugal with the money he made from working as a student, and also from a government student maintenance loan. He was able to invest in learning and applying entrepreneurship and setting up his company. We both built startups that were profitable very quickly, rather than with a monetisation strategy that came later, and neither of us raised funding for our first ventures.

In fact, having a lot of money, like being born with the proverbial silver spoon in your mouth, can make you complacent and less hungry to make money and succeed in your personal life. You have the luxuries already. You have pretty much all your desires met. You're not likely to be driven. And then even if you do start a startup, you'll probably try to solve problems by throwing money at them. For example, you may just start spending thousands a month on marketing from the get-go rather than 'growth scrapping' with innovative and usually more time-consuming 'manual' methods. We'll talk about growth scrapping in Chapter 16 (The Business).

For now, know that financial constraints can breed creativity, resourcefulness and ingenuity while having excessive amounts can breed more wasteful behaviour and lead to a startup's downfall. As the saying goes, 'Necessity is the mother of invention'.

So, if you feel like you weren't 'fortunate' enough to be privileged and have access to money easily, with passive income coming in constantly from rental properties and dividends, then you have to work on other unfair advantages and leverage your creativity and outside-the-box thinking, which we'll talk about more in the next chapter.

8

Intelligence and insight

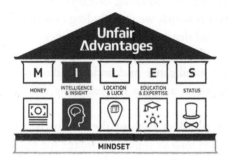

When did someone last call you smart? Do you think of yourself as intelligent?

Growing up, Hasan was often told he was intelligent. He'd do well at school despite not doing his homework and had an intellectual curiosity and ability to wrap his head around concepts and ideas very well.

Ash, on the other hand, says that he wasn't the smartest, but he grew up surrounded by friends who were. He noticed that they often said he was the glue that held them together. Later on in life, he realised the power of the social intelligence he had. His other strength in intelligence is his creativity – Ash has always thought innovatively about how to solve problems.

These are different types of smarts but they all fall under the heading of Intelligence.

Types of intelligence

Intelligence might sound like a pretty straightforward concept at first, but as you study it, it becomes more and more difficult to accurately define. However, we all know what we mean when we describe someone as intelligent.

In fact, intelligence has many dimensions. We are going to cover them in the following categories: IQ, Book Smarts, Street Smarts (in which we're including emotional and social intelligence), and finally Creative Intelligence.

Next, we will move on to Insight, which is a form of deeper, more specific, intelligence and understanding that gives us a unique perspective, and can be absolutely vital for a startup founder.

Let's take a look at each of these in turn, and how they might be turned into an unfair advantage for you as a startup founder, and also in life in general.

Intelligence Quotient

When we talk about intelligence, Intelligence Quotient, or IQ always comes up. Maybe it's the first thing you thought of. IQ testing is a measurement that has been around for over a century as a way to rank people by intelligence: Albert Einstein and Stephen Hawking had IQs of over 160. That means they were pretty damn smart.

But the question remains – does IQ really matter?

The short answer is 'yes'. According to many reputable studies, children who score higher on IQ tests will, *on average*, go on to do better in the conventional measures of success in life: academic achievement, economic success. These children are also more likely to have better health, and a longer life.

The long answer is more complicated. The topic of intelligence (and IQ specifically) has always been controversial, because there is no general agreement on what intelligence actually *is*. Since intelligence can manifest across a broad range of abilities, it is difficult to combine these to reach one global measurement. Which means we can never *really* know.

So, while we see correlations between IQ and success on a broad scale in society, this information is actually not useful to us individually. That's why the previous statement about children scoring higher on IQ tests says 'on average'. That's key. IQ doesn't predict how you'll actually do in your life. For instance, Christopher Langan, considered to be the smartest man in the world, with an incredible IQ score of over 190, worked as a labourer and bouncer for the vast majority of his life. Not what you'd expect.

Most importantly, IQ doesn't actually measure emotional and social intelligence, nor does it factor in self-awareness or creativity.

So while it does have some predictive ability over a large population, so may be useful in policy considerations, for us as *individuals*, IQ is not useful. In fact, in a 2011 meta-analysis by Angela Duckworth, it was found that IQ testing scores were affected by motivation. So participants who were offered cash for a higher test score scored on average 20 points higher! This shows that there are a lot of pitfalls when trying to measure intelligence in this generalised way, and it is not a way we would recommend when auditing yourself.

Is a higher IQ an unfair advantage? Yes.

Is it something to pay much attention to when seeking to get success for yourself? No.

Why? Because while most experts can agree that intelligence is improvable, IQ as a measure in and of itself is widely considered to be out of our control. And there is no general consensus around it.

What's important for us to know is that real leverage in

entrepreneurship largely comes from the things that IQ doesn't test, such as social and emotional intelligence, creativity and self-awareness. After all, business isn't an exam. It's a process. Business success is almost always about relationships and adding value to other people, and assembling and working in a team.

When it comes to IQ, don't let a number define you. If you've never done an IQ test, don't bother. What is far more useful to understand is a concept that virtually all psychologists definitely agree on:

Believing you can get smarter actually makes you smarter.

Book smarts

You can think of book smarts as the capacity for theoretical understanding. It's also a style of learning – some people prefer to increase their knowledge through books and formal education. This type of intelligence gives us conceptual frameworks that we can use as tools for understanding the world.

You probably already have a feeling of whether or not you're 'book smart' based purely on how well you did at school and in exams. Those test how good you are at absorbing large amounts of information. But don't write off your 'book smarts' just because of your early years of life or your performance at academic institutions. You may discover and develop your book smarts later in life because you're getting to do it in a self-directed way.

Ash, for example, didn't do very well in school, but he is now a voracious reader of non-fiction books and content. His interest in the concept allows him to excel at learning the material. When it came to teaching himself to code using books from the library, this quickly became an unfair advantage for him. This is because Ash is a 'why' learner, meaning he needs to know why he's learning something and how it can help him achieve a practical goal. 'Why' learners like Ash often don't do well in school, where the answer to 'why' is simply because it will come up in the exam. (More about learning in Chapter 10: Education and Expertise.)

Have you noticed that the smartest kids in school don't necessarily do that well in life? When you see them at school reunions, for instance, you may find that they aren't doing as well financially as you'd have expected, or if they are, they're not fulfilled by their job and often talk about wanting a career change.

If you enjoy learning from books, and find that you grasp concepts quickly and easily without having to go and do it yourself first, then you've got a really helpful unfair advantage already – books contain all the knowledge accumulated throughout world history, so there will always be something to read and learn from. Equally, when you're founding a startup, it doesn't hurt to have a degree certificate and a string of letters after your name on your CV (though it's by no means essential).

Equally, don't let your exam grades dictate your future success.

Patrick and John Collison – Stripe

One set of startup founders who leveraged their intelligence and book smarts as an unfair advantage are the duo of Patrick and John Collison. Raised in a small village in rural Ireland, the two brothers founded Stripe, a payments processing startup that helps companies take payments online, when they were only 21 and 19 respectively. This little startup went on to make them both billionaires in a few short years and the younger brother John took the crown of Forbes's youngest self-made billionaire in 2016.

Their big unfair advantage is their incredible Intelligence.

Patrick Collison took his first computer course when he was just eight years old, at the University of Limerick, and began studying computer programming at the age of just ten. At sixteen he wowed the judges of the BT Young Scientist of the Year when he came up with a whole new computer programming language which he named Croma. He skipped his last year at school and enrolled at the prestigious Massachusetts Institute of Technology (MIT) in the US.

Younger brother John Collison finished with the highest ever score on his Leaving Certificate, the Irish equivalent of A-levels. In fact, John was accepted into Harvard *before* even taking his final exams.

Following in the footsteps of Bill Gates and Mark Zuckerberg, both Patrick and John dropped out of their respective elite universities to start their company.

Here's what's interesting. Although Stripe is the business the Collison brothers are best known for, they were actually self-made millionaires before Stripe. The startup they founded that gave them that millionaire status was called Auctomatic, and was designed to help eBay sellers manage their transactions and maximise how much money they made. They developed it with Croma, the unique coding language created by Patrick, and they both became millionaires from this startup while they were still teenagers. In fact, John started and exited this startup and became a millionaire before he even went to university!

Here's what John says about studying:

'I'm a bit of a nerd in that one of the reasons I did so many subjects [for the Leaving Certificate] is just that I enjoyed them all. So it's the same with college, I want to take it on to the next level.'

Not only is John smart and conscientious, he absolutely loves studying – similar to Warren Buffett talking about how he tap dances to work every morning. Book smarts is John's learning style. Through his passion for book learning, he's also developed the drive to take things further, to get to the next level. Despite dropping out of college, we can see that he's taken the discipline of studying, and applied it to creating his startup.

So these brothers are just one example of how book smarts and intelligence can get you ahead. But what if you're not into studying?

'Street smarts' and people skills

The stuff you learn outside of school is 'street smarts'. Street smarts are developed by doing. You'll have some kind of baseline 'talent' at it, but ultimately it's developed primarily through real-life experience, and by learning from other people's real-life experiences.

For those of us who are always looking for another unfair advantage, this should be encouraging. Street smarts can be developed through experience. From rolling your sleeves up and getting 'stuck in' to just picking it up every day through observation of how others do things, these first-hand experiences develop your street smarts more than anything else. Having friends or mentors with a lot of experience is also incredibly useful as they guide you to make the right 'street smart' decisions.

Street smarts is largely about people skills, which require emotional and social intelligence. From recruiting your technical co-founder to speaking to potential customers and unearthing their needs, frustrations and goals, from calling that supplier and negotiating costs to getting a loan or investment (if need be), people skills are absolutely essential to every stage of a startup.

A shockingly large proportion of startups fail because the founders have a falling out, or an investor screws them over.

Street smarts earned from being in the game helps prevent this, but so does having the right mentors, advisors and partners to help you steer clear of such fraught situations in the first place.

Emotional intelligence is so vital because business is between people, and as people we are very affected by emotion, more so than logic. If you can read, understand and affect people's emotions positively, you can influence and persuade them. That's how you attract co-founders, mentors, investors and employees to join you in your startup. That's how you negotiate a pay rise. That's how you connect with customers. Emotional intelligence is key.

Street smarts are comprised of three different elements:

1. **Social and emotional intelligence** Knowing which questions to ask, how to ask those questions in a way that gets you the answers you're after, building trust and relationships, and being assertive.

2. **Common sense** Knowing who you can trust, who you should approach, and getting a sense of different trends and the demand for different things.

3. **Bullsh*t detection** Knowing when people are trying to screw you over, reading their intentions, and having a sense of where their incentives lie.

Nikola Tesla: a lack of street smarts

Born in what is now Croatia in 1856, Nikola was an extraordinarily gifted child. He had a knack for doing advanced calculus in his mind, and his teachers couldn't believe that he wasn't somehow cheating. Fascinated by demonstrations of electricity by his science teachers, he essentially dedicated his life to the inventions related to harnessing it.

We can thank Nikola Tesla and his genius not only for

safe, affordable electricity delivered to our homes, but also for radio, robots and remote controls (plus a whole load of other inventions).

However, sadly Nikola died almost penniless for a number of reasons, one of which was his naivety and lack of 'street smarts' when it came to business and social intelligence. For example, Thomas Edison promised him $50,000 if he could redesign his motor and generators to be safer and more efficient, and after a couple of months Tesla went back with a fully functional induction motor running on alternating current. However, when he asked Edison for his money, Edison refused and reportedly quipped 'Tesla, you don't understand our American humor.'

Through Nikola Tesla we can see the importance of street smarts to business success – and how having people skills can often be more important than being incredibly intelligent.

Despite his lack of financial legacy, Nikola Tesla's intellectual legacy is very strong. In fact, he inspired the name of Elon Musk's electric car company: Tesla, Inc. (Elon, of course, is himself a statistical outlier in Intelligence.

Creative intelligence

The final type of intelligence that is a powerful unfair advantage to a startup founder is Creativity.

Although the word is often spoken about in mythological terms, creative ability is not something you're either born with or not. Nor does it only apply in the context of painters and poets. The creativity that we use in day-to-day life and business is all about connecting dots from disparate fields and coming up with unique solutions. Creativity is largely about training your mind to connect things you learn in one domain to situations that seem completely unrelated. This is known as intersectionality.

Not only does coming up with a ground-breaking idea

require creativity, it's also extremely valuable in finding ways to grow a startup ('growth hacking'). This is Ash's main strength, and one of the primary drivers of his success.

Innovation is not a mysterious gift that depends on some kind of 'Eureka!' moment that hits you out of the blue. We all have creativity in us, and we can all develop our creativity – it is a skill we can consciously work on. One way to improve creativity is to increase your interdisciplinary knowledge: Learn from areas and fields of knowledge, and other industries, that are completely different to what you already know. You will learn a lot and develop mental models that are more diverse and that will allow you to think more laterally.

Steve Jobs famously wandered into a calligraphy class when he was at university and learned how to create beautiful, proportionally spaced letters and fonts. Later, when he worked with his designers on the Mac, they completely revolutionised computing with the fonts, beautiful design and elegance, which gave Apple a huge competitive advantage over their rivals Microsoft.

Business in the past was more about incremental improvements, cost savings and efficiency economies in factories. But the future is more about looking at how something is done now, and doing something completely new and innovative. Creativity is already becoming more and more important, as machines and artificial intelligence can't match the human mind when it comes to creativity. This means it will continue to be a very strong unfair advantage into the future, both for entrepreneurship and for people's careers in general.

The importance of insight

Intelligence is useful. Being smart, reading lots, spending time observing and meeting people, transferring your understanding of one discipline to give you the edge in another – all these things will help you advance your startup, and possibly give you the drive to start it in the first place. But for your idea to work, you also need some kind of unique Insight.

By insight we mean being able to see below the surface of things, and to understand elements of a situation that others might not. You might have insight into a particular market, because of your own background, or have insight into an upcoming trend because you've been researching similar products for a while and can see where it's going.

For example, Hasan's insight was the fact that traditional business owners and entrepreneurs had no idea how to market themselves online, and get more customers via the internet. For his latest startup, Ash's insight is the fact that people need to keep upskilling themselves in this new era of accelerating technology, and that we learn better from expert practitioners and in small groups.

Whatever your particular insight, it's undeniably crucial to have the power of insight as a founder of a startup.

Having an insight means finding a need. Finding a gap in the market. Seeing an inconvenience that can be solved. Figuring out the inadequacies or inefficiencies of existing products and services on the market. In other words, finding a real problem to solve.

The key is to spend more time on the problem than on your solution to that problem. Understanding the problem you're solving inside and out is the powerful insight. This is what investors are after.

Paul Graham, investor, startup essayist and co-founder of Y Combinator explains the importance of insight:

> What we look for in ideas is not the type of idea but the level of insight you have about it. It's a common mistake to say

the distinctive thing about your solution will be that it's well-designed and easy to use. That is not an insight. You're just claiming you're going to execute well. Whoever wrote the current software was presumably also trying to. So you have to be more specific. Exactly what are you going to do that will make your software easier to use? And will that be enough?

This applies to any product or service, not just software or an app.

Remember with Ash's story how difficult it was for him to implement payment processing to take payments on his website? The Collison brothers had the insight of making their payment system (Stripe) really easy and convenient for developers to put into their websites and apps. It's so easy to use – just seven lines of code – and they were able to build that to over $20 billion of valuation. This is in contrast to their competitor at the time, Paypal, which was already very established. Paypal, the leading payment platform, focused more on the needs of the customer whereas Stripe had the insight to focus on the needs of the developer.

Steve Jobs had the insight of integrating elegant design-thinking into all of Apple's products.

Jeff Bezos had the insight incredibly early on that the internet was going to change retail forever.

The main way for you to get insight is by talking to potential customers. It's that simple.

If your business idea starts with getting users and not customers, then they're the ones you need to focus on. If your monetisation strategy is trading users' attention for advertising revenue, then their attention is essentially the product that you sell to advertisers (basically how Facebook and Google make money).

It's even better if you're the target customer yourself. This automatically gives you deep insight into their experience.

You'll understand the problem you're trying to solve intimately as you've experienced it first-hand. Nevertheless, be sure to still talk to other people who have the same problem, since you cannot assume that everyone else experiences it to the same extent as you do.

That's why it can be quite a good idea to get a job within an industry. Only by gaining that level of insight from working can you get really valuable insights about pain points and inefficiencies which can be solved through a better product or process. This is why domain expertise in a certain industry can be so valuable. For example, if you work in HR and you see a manual process that could be automated, that manual process is an inconvenience and a problem that can be solved with technology.

Tristan Walker – insight in action

'Humble, raised in Queens. I just got opportunity, got lucky.' This is how Tristan Walker introduced himself in a radio interview.

'Why do you feel like you got lucky? It was a formula? You put the work in?' asked one of the hosts.

'Yeah, I put the work in', Tristan replied, 'but I understand that I'm in the right place at the right time. Fortunately, I've had some people around me supporting me in the right position, and I'm appreciative of it.'

Tristan Walker is the founder of Walker & Co, a beauty brand aimed at people of colour who struggle with razor burn and ingrown hairs. After five years, his startup was bought by Procter & Gamble, the owner of Gillette, for an undisclosed sum, estimated to have been between $20 and $40 million. And he got to carry on as CEO.

Tristan was raised by a single mother in the projects (social housing) in Queens, his father having been shot and killed when he was just three years old. His mother worked three jobs to support her children, and Tristan used to dream of finding his way out.

The black heroes and role models he saw in the media were musicians, entertainers and sports stars, so he tried to become an athlete, but couldn't get into the basketball team. Fortunately for him he was a straight-A student, so one of the coaches recommended he apply for a scholarship to one of the elite boarding schools that his public (state) school used to play against.

This worked: he aced the test and chose one of the best ones in the country, Hotchkiss School in Connecticut. He refers to his time at boarding school as being the four most transformative years of his life.

After excelling at university and graduating top of his class, Tristan landed a Wall Street job through an organisation called Sponsors for Educational Opportunity, which offer training and internship programs for under-represented minorities in business.

The way he describes it is that he had a strong vision and drive to get wealthy. And that's what he saw in that elite boarding school. Wealth. Not just quick money. Not just rich. Rather, old money, serious *wealth*. And that's what he wanted to attain as quickly as possible.

He got a really good job, and then the 2008 recession hit. He lost his job.

The athletic career didn't work out. The Wall Street career didn't either. He only had one other idea: entrepreneurship.

So he went to Stanford, and as it's based at the heart of it and is so thoroughly partnered to it, he 'discovered' Silicon Valley. Kids like him didn't grow up knowing it existed. Through Silicon Valley, he saw 24-year-olds like himself who were already millionaires. This was a lightbulb moment for him.

This was the early days of Twitter, and Tristan saw the impact that this startup was beginning to have. So he decided to do an internship there when they only had twenty staff. This gave him incredible insights and exposure to the startup world.

Then he noticed Foursquare, a location-based app which was just starting to show traction, and he reached out to the CEO. Foursquare was based in New York so when the CEO finally replied with a hint of interest, he immediately jumped on a plane and went to work there.

He was their director of business development and their first employee.

Tristan built his commercial and selling skills at Foursquare, then became an entrepreneur-in-residence at the legendary Andreesen Horowitz, one of the most famous and influential venture capital firms, and was mentored by Ben Horowitz, one of the partners.

He stayed there for nine months, trying to come up with a BIG startup idea, and considered tackling obesity, banking and even fixing freight and trucking.

But his most important insight, the one that sits at the heart of his business and sets it apart from other beauty startups, came from himself. As an African American man dealing with razor burn and ingrown hairs on a day-to-day basis, he realised that people like him, with coarse, curly hair, were not being catered to directly by any existing company when it came to shaving.

This was his 'Aha' moment. This was his idea and unique insight.

Tristan's unfair advantage was that he was the target customer of his own startup. He was solving his own problem so had key insights into the pain points of this customer segment.

Deliveroo – working for insight

Tristan Walker's example of coming up with an idea to scratch your own itch is just one path to success. You can also solve problems for target markets that you are not part of, as long as you spend a hell of a lot of time speaking to them and gathering intelligence into what their fears and frustrations are, their pain points, and their dreams and desires, their aspirations.

When Will Shu founded his company Deliveroo, he was initially also his own target market – but in the process of becoming an entrepreneur, he realised that he would have to dig deeper to understand all the problems his customers faced.

Shu had been a banker at Morgan Stanley in New York. Working 100-hour weeks, he was used to getting food delivered to the office. When he was transferred to London, he found the meal delivery in the UK's capital to be severely lacking compared to New York. There was clearly a gap in the market for an accessible, fast and comprehensive delivery service. This insight came to him because of his unique position working long hours in both cities. However, Will Shu developed an even stronger Insight Ð one he had to work for.

Once he had founded Deliveroo, he decided to ride his bike around as a delivery guy himself, 8 hours a day, 7 days a week, for 9 months when he first launched! Most wealthy founders would never bother working so hard at something for which they could easily hire someone. However, he wanted to understand the logistics of food delivery first hand. Not only did he gain insights about the challenges for the delivery riders working for him, he was also able to glean valuable information from the restaurants, and from other couriers. They didn't know he was the founder and CEO, so he was doing it like an undercover boss. Most crucially, he gained insights from the customers themselves. He was able to see all the possible obstacles and difficulties from end-to-end. This is something that few entrepreneurs are willing to do, to roll their sleeves up and get their hands dirty to such an extent.

(Will Shu's former colleagues actually used to use Deliveroo in the early days purely to see the former banker reduced to being a delivery boy. There was even an occasion when he delivered to a posh house in Knightsbridge only to have the occupant look at him in shock – he realised he used to work with Shu in banking, and thought that he must have fallen on really hard times.)

Shu wasn't so far removed from his target market, but even then he had to work for his Insights. You might want to start a business that's even further removed from your own current situation, and if so, there's nowhere better to start in gathering information than by getting out there and talking to all the people your product will involve and serve.

Intelligence and insight as your unfair advantage

Just as with the unfair advantage of Money, you probably already have a good sense of whether or not you're above average in Intelligence, especially when it comes 'book smarts'. Over the course of your life, people will probably have told you that you're smart and you'll have the grades to prove it. If you're concerned about a lack of intelligence in this sense, then you're actually more likely to be struggling with Education (Chapter 11) or self-confidence, which comes under Status (Chapter 12). You can always read more books, hone your skills and improve your self-belief.

However, when it comes to 'street smarts' – social and emotional intelligence, and even creativity – you may not have had as much feedback in your life, and may not be sure if these are part of your abilities. This is particularly true because for most of us, these kinds of intelligence are hardly assessed at all in school and university, or at least not obviously.

And so you have to assess them yourself, or ask close friends and colleagues for their feedback. Ask:

▶ Can you get a good gut feeling of what other people's intentions are? In other words, can you often sense if somebody has bad intentions?

▶ How well do you work in teams?

▶ How good are you in your interpersonal relationships?

▶ Do you make others around you feel better about themselves?

▶ Are you in touch with your own emotions?

These kinds of questions help you get a sense of where you are. For more depth, try taking an online personality test like the Big 5 we mentioned in the Mindset chapter, or the Myers-Briggs test, and seeing what you get for things connected to social intelligence.

If you realise, through thinking about your behaviour, talking to others, and assessing your personality, that you are not the most 'people person' then it's not a disaster. First of all, as we've said elsewhere, you may want to consider getting a co-founder who compliments you – someone who loves working in a team, is very sociable and emotionally attuned. Then, there are plenty of management courses you can go on, as well as books like Dale Carnegie's *How to Win Friends and Influence People*, that will help you to improve your relations. Even just the first step of considering these things will make you more aware of them, and probably improve your relationships.

When it comes to creativity and insight, you have to consider how good you are at coming up with creative solutions to problems. Do you relish challenges and puzzles, and try to solve them? Are you observant and curious about your environment, the people around you, and how people feel? Do you notice when you encounter inconveniences and problems in day-to-day life yourself? Do you consider how they could be solved?

To develop your Intelligence and Insight, you have to:

1. Cultivate your curiosity.
2. Ask more questions.
3. Do more experiments.
4. Be more interested in how people *feel*, and the emotional impact things have on them.
5. Notice when people say something is a pain to do, or is inconvenient. These are goldmines for valuable insights (more about this in Chapter 14 – The Idea).
6. Be more aware of your own emotions and moods, and don't let them dictate your actions.

Intelligence and insight as a double-edged sword

Like all unfair advantages, intelligence is a double-edged sword. A lack of intelligence (or perceived intelligence) can actually make you more willing to hire or outsource to people who are 'intelligent'. It might make you willing to ask questions, and actually listen to the answers – to find experts and practitioners who can guide and help you. Though you might not be the person with the most intelligence or insight, you might develop the team-building skills necessary to accomplish the same result. Richard Branson explains this as his path to success. As someone who struggled in school (and later found out he had dyslexia), he learned from a young age to delegate to those who were 'smarter' than him. That way, he learned valuable management and people skills.

Equally, a high intelligence can be a barrier to success in

some cases. Why? Because that big brain can foresee all the obstacles and difficulties. Someone with a high intelligence might see fifty different paths into the future and find problems with all of them. Many founders say that with hindsight, if they had known how difficult it would be, they might not have done it. Looking back, however, they are glad that they did it anyway. You need a bit of foolishness to become a startup founder.

Similarly, deep insight based purely on your own experience (when scratching an itch for yourself) can be misleading, as you may be one of only a handful of people with this exact issue. So without validating your idea, you may spend a lot of time and money solving something that isn't a problem for most people, and therefore has very little potential as a startup idea. It's why it's so important to get out and work for your insight.

9

Location and luck

'The two most important requirements for major success are: first, being in the right place at the right time, and second, doing something about it.' Ray Kroc, pioneer of McDonald's

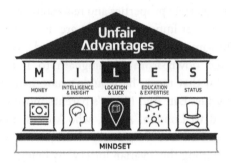

How did this book end up in your hands? Probably through a series of serendipitous events. For example, even its authors did not meet through a mutual friend. We didn't happen to work at the same company. Neither one was a client of the other. The way we met, and how this book ended up in your hands, is down to pure chance. We both went to a business dinner, which is not something either of us make a habit of doing, we ended up sitting next to each other and joked about the quality of the overpriced steak in front of us. Then, at the end of the event, it just so happened that we found that we lived in the same part of London. Then this fact meant that

Hasan would drop by Ash's office and a friendship and investment partnership built from there and led to us writing this book which you're now holding in your hands.

Serendipity matters. Location and Luck mean being in the right place at the right time.

Let's start with Location, because being in the right location increases your chances of luck.

Location

Location may seem pretty meaningless until you realise how powerful it really is. In properties and real estate, it's often said that the three most important factors are: location, location, location. The same is often true for people and businesses.

Ash moved down from Birmingham to London. If it hadn't been for that move, he wouldn't have had the opportunity to join Just Eat. And Hasan's parents moved with him from Baghdad to London. Again, who knows how his life would have turned out if he'd stayed there. Warren Buffett mentioned winning the 'ovarian lottery' by being born in the United States. These are all elements of location and luck.

When it comes to businesses, we're always interested to see which of the shops on our local high street come and go. Over the years, businesses have opened and closed regularly. It seems some locations just don't work, no matter the business.

But does location itself hold so much power for businesses, or is it all about how good the business is itself?

If your boutique clothes shop, for example, is in the middle of nowhere, you're not likely to make many sales. If your new gym is based in a geographically hard-to-reach place, it will be tough to get many customers.

It's pretty obvious. If your physical business is in a bad location, customers are less likely to stumble upon it, or make the journey to use your facilities.

That's why there are such things as shopping centres or high streets, where you'll find so many similar businesses competing with each other in the same place. That's also why there's such a thing as a restaurant and nightlife district, again with businesses all competing with each other. Or what about Chinatowns in cities all over the world? Why would all Chinese restaurants compete with each other on the same patch of land?

Clearly there must be benefits to being in a certain place that outweigh the downside of competition, or increased cost. This phenomenon is called 'clustering' in economics – that businesses tend to cluster together.

The question is, why does clustering occur? Why do businesses seem to cluster together, even when they are direct competitors, and even when the product the business is selling doesn't rely on customers who are geographically close?

Let's look at some examples:

Hollywood, Bollywood, Savile Row, Wall Street, the City, Fleet Street, Harley Street, Silicon Valley, Silicon Roundabout, and Sand Hill Road.

What do all of these have in common?

They're metonyms, which means they're not just the name of a place, they have come to be shorthand references for whole industries. Hollywood and Bollywood for their film industries, Savile Row for quality tailored suits, Wall Street and the City (of London) for banking and finance, Fleet Street for the media (despite most newspapers not being based there since the 1980s), Harley Street for private doctors and top consultants, Silicon Valley and Silicon Roundabout (more officially known as London Tech City) for technology companies, and Sand Hill Road (which is in Silicon Valley) for venture capitalists.

But isn't it better to be where there is less competition?

Sometimes, but competition is not the only factor. For a prime example of clustering, let's talk about the world's undisputed king of the startup, Silicon Valley.

The Silicon Valley story

This relatively small geographic area in northern California is home to three out of five of the most valuable companies in the world – Google, Apple and Facebook – plus literally tens of thousands of startups. For decades Silicon Valley has been where you go to set up a technology startup ('silicon' originally referred to the large number of silicon chip innovators and manufacturers in the region), and now increasingly any type of startup, not just tech.

But how did it all start? Similar to how success is attained by individuals through the accumulation of unfair advantages, Silicon Valley originally emerged as a tech startup hub because of a confluence of factors. It starts with geography. San Francisco port helped make it a US navy base and a research airfield was established in the Valley, so a number of technology startups were set up in the area to serve the navy. This is way back in the 1930s by the way, when a computer was the size of a room. NASA later moved into the area, again increasing the number of researchers, technologists and engineers in the Valley, mainly in the aerospace industry.

The fact that there were world-class STEM (Science, Technology, Engineering and Mathematics) research universities in the area, like Stanford, also really helped, especially in providing a highly skilled talent pool of graduates. However, at the time most of this talent would move away to get jobs. It was a Stanford professor, Frederick Terman, who wanted to create jobs in the area so that graduates didn't have to move away to find employment. He decided to do this by leasing new land owned by Stanford to anyone who wanted to set up high-tech startups. His biggest success was being able to convince his mentees William Hewlett and David Packard to establish their startup there. You may have heard of their company, Hewlett Packard, now simply known as HP.

Other factors were more serendipitous: London-born American innovator William Shockley had moved his semiconductor company all the way from New Jersey on the east coast to Silicon Valley in the 1950s, simply to look after his ailing mother. His breakthrough innovations in semiconductors later helped spur on the tech industry even further.

This increasing number of innovative high-tech startups, centred around Stanford University, really kicked the growth of this ecosystem into high gear in the 1970s, when venture capitalists like Kleiner Perkins and Sequoia Capital started to set up shop on Sand Hill Road in the Valley, to fund the next big thing. Available VC money skyrocketed after Apple Computer's $1.3 billion IPO in 1980.

The availability of funding, of engineers, and also an effect called 'knowledge spillover' was the perfect storm to make Silicon Valley the dominant region for the startup ecosystem. Knowledge spillover is basically how information, knowledge and insights spread informally between different firms, merely because they are near one another. This could happen through simple things such as friendships, roommates, and employees moving from one company to another and then sharing technical and business insights and innovations from their previous company.

You can see that Silicon Valley's world superiority as a startup ecosystem is a fantastic illustration of how unfair advantages can accumulate and create a virtuous circle (a positive feedback loop) that grows and grows at an accelerating rate. In 2017, almost 45 per cent of all US venture capital investment went into this small geographical area.

This clustering is not unique to the US (which also has other clusters in Boston, Seattle, New York and Austin).

Startup clusters

In the UK, we have 'Silicon Roundabout' in London, and 'Silicon Fen' in Cambridge (sometimes referred to as The Cambridge Cluster), as well as Oxford Science Park, and other centres like Manchester, Edinburgh and Bristol. Again these are clustered around top universities where talent and funding are available.

To show how disproportionately active a tech hub like London is compared to the rest of the UK, London and Partner (a government agency) recently published research that showed that 75 per cent of money raised by the country's tech sector was pumped into fledgling businesses *within the capital itself.*

These hubs are a worldwide phenomenon. There's Berlin, Bangalore, Beijing, Shenzhen and Singapore. (Indonesia is also interesting as it has the hubs of Jakarta, Bandung and Yogyakarta, but also the famous digital nomad hub in Bali, where entrepreneurs work on their laptops from beach-side bars.)

So being based in one of these powerful location hubs can be a real unfair advantage, with access to investors, highly skilled labour, and insight and knowledge (or just beautiful and inexpensive sun, sea and sand in Bali). You also get the infrastructure you need in these hubs, such as fast internet connections.

This cluster effect does not last forever though – in the case of Silicon Valley, increased crowding in the Valley and very high wages has led to skyrocketing costs of living which in turn have forced many young companies to move to alternative locations such as Austin, Texas.

The same thing has happened in Silicon Roundabout in London, as rents have shot up in what used to be quite inexpensive parts of London – Hoxton, Old Street and Shoreditch.

So, these startup hubs are spurred on by top STEM and Business universities, but also benefit greatly from being surrounded by like-minded entrepreneurs and hustlers who are working hard to solve problems, create solutions, and become millionaires out of it.

Location affects the vibe that you're infected with. It's said that you become the average of the five people you spend the most time with, so being surrounded by innovative and entrepreneurial people, who are ambitious and hardworking, is likely to have a positive effect on your own ambitions, attitudes and productivity. One of the most significant things we noticed when we visited Silicon Valley was that they think BIG. They are more confident and more ambitious than virtually anywhere else in the world when it comes to startups. There are also more relevant events and meetups in startup hubs which, again, helps you.

Equally though, location doesn't have to be purely physical. Location is also your environment, and online we have a lot more control over how we carve and design our environment through who we follow and befriend on social media, and through what type of content we consume. Having the right type of people around you and joining entrepreneurial groups and masterminds is incredibly valuable.

We are social creatures and we're strongly influenced by our environments. One of the biggest 'hacks' or shortcuts to personal growth and development is via those we spend our time with. So, even if you're thinking of creating a startup that doesn't need a local customer base, it's worth taking your location into consideration.

While moving your startup to an area like Silicon Valley, London or Bangalore can have a positive impact on your staff, your ideas and your access to funding, picking a location with a recognisable reputation can also help you in other ways. Location can imply Status because of the prestige associated with certain areas (usually areas which are expensive). If you say you're making your film in Hollywood, people are likely to take you more seriously. If you're looking for a top doctor, you'll be reassured if they work in Harley Street. And if someone hands you their business card and their office is somewhere super fancy, you're likely to be impressed. One person who understood the importance and has reaped the benefits of an address is James Caan. Today Caan is a successful entrepreneur, investor, and former dragon on *Dragon's Den*, but when he was starting his first business, he had a choice to make: where should he put the office?

Instead of renting a cheaper property, he chose an office in Mayfair for the unconscious biases tied to that super-expensive location. Never mind the room was so small he couldn't open it without hitting his desk. Never mind the fact he would have to have meetings with potential clients elsewhere. Caan knew at that point in his career that an address in Mayfair would make his company look bigger than it actually was. His success in that first endeavour would act as a springboard for the rest of his career.

For James Caan, his physical address mattered to his clients, almost as much as a high-street shop's. But does that apply to online businesses as well?

Yes, this time in the form of search engine rankings. Being at the top of Google search results, for instance, gets you more website visitors. This is because of the combined effect of customers' laziness (they don't want to scroll through pages of results) and your implied quality and Status through being at the top (which suggests you're more trustworthy and more useful).

In the early days of Just Eat, when we were based in Edgware, it was tougher to find the talent willing to make that commute to the suburb. Once we paid a little more for the Silicon Roundabout location, the highly skilled people who came on board far outweighed the cost of the increased rent.

In London, you have access to all the conferences, seminars, panels, and other cutting-edge trends that you don't have elsewhere. Even though you'll have to compromise in some areas by moving to a smaller space, the ease of getting to top people, talent, and information might be worth that sacrifice to you.

In summary, location can give you access to capital (investors and venture capital firms tend to cluster in startup hubs) and to highly skilled talent.

Huda Kattan – move to where your audience is

Huda Kattan is the founder of Huda Beauty, which is estimated at one billion dollars, while her own fortune is estimated at half a billion dollars. In 2017, she sold a minority stake in her business to a private equity firm. This makes her the first social media beauty influencer to attract private equity money.

Huda was born in Oklahoma to Iraqi immigrant parents, an engineering professor father and a full-time mother, and began using beauty products aged just nine. She talks about how she felt unattractive as a young girl, and so was always deeply interested in makeup. She loved experimenting with cosmetics and DIY beauty hacks with her three sisters in her spare time.

She was obsessed with makeup but didn't realise it could be a career.

She studied business at university. She was interested in finance and loved dealing with numbers. However, once she graduated and started working in financial recruitment, she realised she had no passion for it.

At a loss of what to do, and having been made redundant from her job, Huda was encouraged by her family to go to makeup school. She went to the top makeup school in the US, Joe Blasco in Los Angeles, and absolutely loved it.

While she was there, she began blogging. Every day she would go to college, come back home and blog, then go out in the evening to socialise, have fun, network and get her face out there.

(Notice the extraversion, the conscientiousness and the diligence.)

She followed this intense routine for a long time, but she enjoyed it at the same time.

In the first year, she had almost zero traction with her blog. However, after working hard and eventually working her way up to being a makeup artist to celebrity clients like Eva Longoria and Nicole Richie, she decided to move to Dubai. With her darker, middle-eastern look, more geared to the middle-eastern makeup aesthetic, she felt she would have more impact.

(Location: going to where her initial audience and target market was.)

With the encouragement of her sister, she decided to launch her first product in her brand, false lashes. Her sister invested $6,000 and they went for it, with Huda being very particular about the look and feel of the brand, the packaging, and the quality of product, responding to a particular need for women who wanted beautiful false lashes.

Her lashes were so successful that Kim Kardashian herself began wearing them.

(Insight: she knew exactly the branding and the product specifications that her audience would like. Status: she was so good that she was doing makeup for celebrities, royals, and then having her products used by the celebrity-royal that is Kim Kardashian.).

Her vision was to get into the beauty emporium Sephora in Dubai mall, and with a lot of hiccups and obstacles on the way, she got there. She attributes a lot of her success to the tough skin she developed when she was being cyber-bullied.

(Mindset: a strong Vision, developed as she went along.)

We've highlighted the different unfair advantages that Huda Kattan developed and used throughout her career, but the reason we're discussing her success here is because her key Unfair Advantage was Location. Firstly, not only did Huda go to makeup school, she went to *the top makeup school in the United States*. This school also just happened to be in Los Angeles – a hot-bed for potential customers, Hollywood celebrities, and those who wanted to look (and feel) famous and glamorous. She wouldn't have been working with Eva Longoria and Nicole Richie if she'd stayed in Oklahoma. But she also might have remained a behind-the-scenes makeup artist if she'd stayed in LA. Her decision to move to Dubai, where she recognised a broader market for her style and product, allowed her to become a world-renowned brand. And reading her story again after you've understood all the Unfair Advantages in the MILES Framework, you'll spot even more.

Amazon – find the place that has it all

Jeff Bezos founded Amazon in Seattle back in 1994, even though he was working on Wall Street in New York. He had three main reasons for choosing Seattle: one, he wanted access to engineering talent. Seattle was home to the tech behemoth of the time, Microsoft, so anyone looking to make a move to join his startup wouldn't have to move. Second, taxes. He took advantage of a loophole to pay less sales tax by moving there.

Third, distribution. Jeff started selling books only and didn't have his own warehouse, so he wanted to be close to the largest book distribution warehouses to make faster deliveries.

Basecamp – let go of the office obsession

Basecamp is a successful and interesting software startup. Founders Jason Fried and David Heinemeier Hansson really hate a lot of the Silicon Valley hyper-growth, chasing-unicorns, balls-to-the-wall hustle culture.

They started off in a similar way to Hasan, by having a service-based, digital, lifestyle business – a web design agency. David was in Copenhagen, Denmark and Jason was in Chicago.

As they got more clients, it was difficult to manage projects through email chains, and their insight was that they needed one place to put all the information and files for a project in order to be able to manage it properly.

They created some software to use within their company to help with internal project management, and clients started asking them about it. They wanted to use it themselves. That's when they started becoming a software company.

They bootstrapped, never raised money from outside investors, and simply grew the business based on revenue.

Jason and David are a great example of a company that was very deliberate about its location, in that the founders and most of their staff live in separate countries. Rather than moving everyone to one place, they've embraced their various locations as a positive, and turned this into a defining feature. They have been able to leverage remote working as a culture in the company.

As they explain:

Over the last 18 years we've been working at making Basecamp a calm company.

And yet we've been profitable every year since the beginning. We've kept our company intentionally small – we believe small is a key to calm. As a tech company we're supposed to be playing the hustle game in Silicon Valley, but we're blissfully far away in Chicago with employees working remotely in 30 different towns around the world.

We each put in about 40 hours a week most of the year, and just 32-hour four-day weeks in the summer. We send people on month-long sabbaticals every three years. We not only pay for people's vacation time, but we pay for the actual vacation too. We're in one of the most competitive industries in the world. An industry dominated by giants and frequent upstarts backed by hundreds of millions of dollars in VC money. We've taken zero. Where does our money come from? Our customers. They buy what we're selling and we treat them exceptionally well. Call us old fashioned.

Luck

I've found that luck is quite predictable. If you want more luck, take more chances. Be more active. Show up more often. Brian Tracy, Canadian motivational speaker

No matter how much skill and determination you have, if you roll a zero for luck, the outcome is zero.
Paul Graham, co-founder of Y Combinator

You may want to know why luck and location are in the same chapter. We actually went back and forth on this, but there was a phrase that we kept returning to:

'Being in the right place at the right time.'

We have discussed Luck in this book already, but it's worth coming back to look at it in the context of right place and right time. Timing is so incredibly important in startups, so the question is, is there something we can do to increase our chances of getting the timing right?

Next, we'll discuss how we can actually increase our chances of getting lucky in general, just by changing our mindset. Sounds too good to be true, but it actually has scientific backing.

Getting the timing right

In the late 1990s, Bill Gross started Idealab – one of the first startup incubators. Naturally he wanted a few questions answered. Mainly he wanted to know what exactly made the difference between successful startups and failures.

In his research, Bill and his team isolated Idealab's top five performing startups and compared them to five startups they had felt extremely optimistic about, but which had ultimately folded. Assuming all the startups he examined had ample funding, he looked at their differences based on three factors:

▶ Timing
▶ Team and execution
▶ Idea

Bill Gross believed the uniqueness of the idea must have been the key factor in whether a startup succeeded or failed. The research showed a different story. The idea actually ranked last of the three. Team and execution finished second. **Timing finished first.**

'The number one thing was timing. Timing accounted for 42 per cent of the difference between success and failure ... Now, this isn't absolutely definitive, it's not to say that the idea isn't important, but it very much surprised me that the idea wasn't the most important thing. Sometimes it mattered more when it was actually timed.'

One of Bill's early companies, a website called GoTo.com (later rebranded as Overture), was the first ever PPC (pay per click) search engine. Initially he thought the success of the site came from the potency of the idea. Looking back, he credits it mostly to timing. He also credits Google's success to timing.

This shows us how essential the right timing is for a startup.

While you can't change the timing of your birth, you can at least have a little bit of control over the timing of your startup. Timing in founding a startup is all about trying to ride the big waves (not short-term trends or hype) that we are being carried on by societal and technological shifts. It's all about the macro trends.

For example, Evan Spiegel and his co-founders had the insight that there was a societal shift for young people of their generation (Generation-Z) to express themselves and communicate visually, with a selfie. This coincided with the technological trend of high-quality front-facing cameras on smartphones which are always connected to the internet through mobile data. They nailed the timing, and that can be partly attributed to the timing of their births, in the sense that they were part of that younger generation themselves.

Another example of great timing is Just Eat, which came about just as, technologically, smartphones and apps were taking off and as, societally, people were becoming less and less inclined to speak to people on the phone (and speak their order to the restaurant), instead gravitating more to simply placing their order using a website or app. Just Eat's IPO came at exactly the right time as well, as they were the first to be listed on the London Stock Exchange's tech-friendly high-growth segment. This really helped them to gain a valuation that was even higher than expected (IPOs are all about timing).

With timing, you can either be too early, too late, or just right.

As an example of being too early, Virtual Reality (VR) has had a lot of hype over the last few years. It seemed like a trend ready to explode back in 2014 when Facebook acquired Oculus, the startup that developed the Oculus Rift, a virtual reality headset, for $2 billion. Personally, since then, we've received endless pitches and pitchdecks of VR and AR startups who wanted to raise funding, emboldened by Oculus's success. However, in 2019, VR still seems like a technology that's too early for mainstream adoption, with heavy bulky headsets and many people experiencing some nausea while using it. We're sure this trend will come, it's just too early.

Being too early or the first to market is bad because you have to educate your potential users and customers about the benefits. Educating the market is a very costly marketing exercise, which makes it very challenging.

Too late, on the other hand, is the case of a startup that's entering a market already too full with competitors – a market that has seen explosive growth in the past. This means you're entering an industry which had a lot of promise and success stories, but where much of its growth has already peaked. Remember when we said it wouldn't be possible to mirror Google's success with a search engine today? It's because search engines are already in this 'too late' scenario. Only with something revolutionary would it be possible.

The ideal situation is to target a small but growing market. This means you've stepped into an industry at exactly the right time. All the unicorns, like those mentioned above, are perfect examples of this: Google, Amazon, Facebook, Netflix, etc.

So that's timing, but can you really change your *luck*? Meaning, can you increase the moments of fortune regardless of your time of birth? Is there some sort of secret for stumbling into good situations?

According to psychologist Dr Richard Wiseman, you can. According to his research, it's largely a matter of mindset. In other words: your thoughts create the luck in your life. If you think you are a lucky person, then you are more likely to experience good fortune. If you think you are an unlucky person, chances are you will experience more ill fortune. So, in this way, you can actually create more luck. More practical advice about how to do this can be found at the end of the chapter, including our own advice on how to increase your luck.

Before the practical advice, let's take a look at a few examples of luck, timing and location.

Nintendo – grab hold of historic moments

From around the end of the eighteenth century, the Japanese government started to bring in strict regulations on gambling. This meant that whenever a card game got very popular, those in power would crack down hard, removing the game and scattering those who played it. By the late 1800s, though, those strict regulations started to ease. The government accepted Nintendo founder Fusajiro Yamauchi's Hanafuda ('flower cards'). However, Japan still banned foreign playing cards from entering the market.

What did this mean? It meant that Yamauchi was able to deliver a game into a game-starved world. He was lucky enough to be born at the exact moment to take advantage of a historic gap in the market, an opportunity that had been suppressed for past entrepreneurs, and wouldn't exist for future competitors. He saw that moment, and grasped it in time for his cards to be consumed by nearly everyone in Japan.

That perfect timing launched a business that continues to exist two centuries later – a fact which can also be put down to the excellent games they've put out since, anticipating and creating the trends of the times: Mario, Zelda and Pokémon continue to do extremely well in the video gaming industry.

Deliveroo – have your idea ready for the right moment

Launched in London, Will Shu knew Deliveroo would work because he could see the problem every day: people wanted food, but they didn't want to go out and get it. Having experienced easy takeaway culture in New York, he could see how a similar project might work in the UK. We saw in the previous chapter how this Insight proved such an important unfair advantage for Deliveroo, but here we see that Location and Luck played their part too. Even though the service it provides is similar to that of Just Eat, Deliveroo was still able to succeed at taking some of the same market. Rather than go for people who wanted food in general, Shu focused on *only* higher-end restaurants, and *only* those who didn't already deliver.

Why did this work? In part because Will Shu started his business in the heart of one of the wealthier parts of London – Chelsea. This was a great location for what he was trying to do, as he knew he could target customers wealthy enough to afford the expensive eating spots. Like New York, the capital city was full of cash-rich, time-poor diners who wanted their food delivered to their door, or office.

In addition, this is also a great example of Timing. Will had initially conceived the idea for Deliveroo way back in 2004, but didn't launch until 2013. What happened? Well, unlike with the initial Just Eat business model, Will envisioned a fleet of couriers to shuttle food to customers, and he wanted to be able to track them. The problem? The technology for that and for tablets was not available yet! When the tech did arrive, Shu was ready to put his ideas into action. There were no other competitors in London yet, and so he got there first. Although he had to wait a whopping nine years before launching, Will Shu lead Deliveroo to unicorn status when the company finally came to be.

Location and luck as your unfair advantage

We all know that location is important. When choosing a place to live, we'll consider all the amenities in the local area – the schools, the transport links, the parks or local gyms – as well as other factors, like the crime rate, whether we like how the area looks, and what's going on in the local community. So why wouldn't we give the same care and attention to where we start our business?

Location may feel like the unfair advantage that we have the least control over (we can't choose where we're born), but it can also be the one that has most potential for flexibility: you can always move!

Only you can know what your business needs, so ask yourself: could your location be better? Before you launch, it's always worth asking yourself if you are positioned – both physically and online – where you need to be in order to give your business the best chance of success.

▶ Are you near other, similar businesses?
▶ Do you have access to the talent you need to build your business?
▶ Are you easy to find for potential clients or customers?

Consider the way your location supports or hinders your progress as a business. You might be hidden away in a residential area, but that might be great for keeping your talented workforce happy living nearby. You might be squeezed into a tiny office, but your prestigious address impresses potential clients.

Even if you're a one-person business, you can think about this – working from home might cut your commute, but staying in your pyjamas all day might affect your productivity. Paying for a desk in a co-working space could impact your profits but increase your network. Weigh up the pros and cons, and see if Location could be the key to your success.

If you feel that your physical location isn't strong, then you have two choices. Either you can move, or you can simply learn to leverage the internet by working and hiring people from all over the world to work with you remotely (as Basecamp did).

In this way, it's also important to consider your location on the internet: is your website inviting? What is its ranking? Investing in good SEO and a strong design are keys here. If your website is one that people want to return to, then you immediately have an unfair advantage over the generic, clunky sites offering similar services.

How to get more lucky

So that's location, which seems relatively simple compared to that fickle thing called luck.

But it is possible to make Luck your Unfair Advantage too. We've already talked about psychologist Dr Richard Weisman's theory that you can create your own luck. So what does that mean in practice?

In his book *The Luck Factor*, Wiseman identifies four basic principles that lucky people use to create good fortune in their lives:

1. Maximise your chance opportunities
In this step, Wiseman says it's not enough to be in the right

place at the right time, you also have to be in the right state of mind for it. He conducted an interesting experiment to illustrate this. Two volunteers, Martin who described himself as lucky, and Brenda, who considered herself unlucky, were asked to wait for further instructions in a coffee shop. The idea was to present each of them with the same opportunities and see how they responded. Wiseman left a five-pound note on the floor for each of them to find, and planted a successful businessman on one of the tables.

The results? Martin noticed and picked up the five-pound note and sat down next to the successful businessman. Within minutes he'd struck up a conversation and even offered to buy him a coffee.

Brenda walked straight past the five-pound note without noticing it, and even though she sat down next to the businessman, she just sat there in silence.

When asked later about their luck that morning, Martin excitedly spoke about how he'd found money on the ground and had met the most interesting person, whereas Brenda just looked blank and said she'd had an uneventful morning. This shows how important it is to always be looking for opportunities, and always be looking to create them. By being observant, proactive and initiating conversation, Martin was able to strike up a friendly relationship with a stranger who could potentially add value to his life. By being more passive, Brenda missed out on this. This is something that natural extroverts would be better at, but even the introverts among us can work at being more open to opportunities and encounters.

2. Trust your intuition and gut feeling, especially when you've had some experience

In a survey of over 100 self-described 'lucky' and 'unlucky' people, over 90 per cent of the lucky ones said they trusted their gut in personal relationships, and over 80 per cent for career decisions. This is because the unconscious mind is surprisingly accurate at noticing patterns, and using past experience to inform present situations. For example, certain body language cues can make you distrust someone, and that could be because you know they're lying.

However, be careful of taking this too far, as unconscious biases and prejudice can form in the same way. There are also many things in business and startups which are counter-intuitive. So you can trust your intuition up to a point, but it's also worth being aware when it's dominating your actions. Another way of saying this is: trust in your abilities and be resourceful.

3. Expect to be lucky

Self-fulfilling prophecies are real. That's why Martin is more likely to notice the money. You'll be more likely to notice opportunities if you try to, and expect to, notice them. This is also part of optimism, which is very powerful.

Ask yourself: where have you had lucky breaks in the past?

We've all had some luck in our lives, and it's important to think about it and be grateful for it, and even expect to be lucky more often.

4. Turn even the bad luck into good luck

Things happen. There are obstacles and challenges along the way to any goal – you can't control this. What you can control is how you view them, and how they impact you. If you get a piece of bad luck, and you sit down and give up, then that's your choice – that action is what makes the event bad. But you could also take it as a learning opportunity and a way to do better next time. You might find a new path, a better goal – how lucky that you got that nudge!

You can make your good luck by focusing your attention

on what you're grateful for, instead of what you don't have. In other words, having a mindset of gratitude and making the most of a situation that you're in. Looking on the bright side.

Ask yourself: have you ever had something bad happen to you which turned out to in fact be a blessing and something good?

Again, this is universal. Our short-sighted perspectives in our own lives can never anticipate where things may lead.

So, obviously, we don't have full control over luck, but we can stack the deck in our favour a bit by having the right mindset.

What we'd add to these four basic principles is very important:

Take more action.

Do more things. Meet more people. Go to more events. Blog about your startup. Produce things and publish them. Get feedback. Put more stuff out into the world. This is a very powerful way of increasing your luck, because it's like trying to roll a double six on a pair of dice, and you can roll as many times as you like. Obviously, you'd just keep rolling the dice until you got a double six. That's increasing your chances, because nobody is counting your number of attempts in life.

Location and luck as a double-edged sword

The flipside of a good 'hub' location is the fact that it can be very expensive. Elsewhere, you can get staff at a lower cost, cheaper office space, lower living costs, etc. All these things can massively help with reducing your burn rate and increasing your runway. Also, just as with Basecamp and digital nomads that travel the world, you can use a non-hub location as a reason to increase your skills at hiring and working remotely, and a way of attracting highly skilled staff who don't already live in your own area. This can be a very powerful way of keeping overheads and staff costs low, and still accessing a huge talent pool of highly skilled workers.

A 'bad' location like a smaller city without much of a startup ecosystem can actually be an advantage. You might see problems and unmet needs here that those in the heart of a metropolis might never find, or where there might be too much competition. With lower costs of living, your startup can survive for much longer before you turn a profit. Moreover, you now have the incentive to work with people all over the world remotely, hence tapping into the worldwide labour market instead of trying to recruit someone from down the street.

But what if you're in Silicon Valley or the Silicon Roundabout in London? Will you find disadvantages there? Yes. A great location can be prohibitively expensive to rent property, or the talent there might be extremely expensive and fickle. Why? They are constantly being courted by other startups to work for them instead.

When it comes to luck, not enough of it means you are all the more determined to do things the hard way. Not lucky enough to be born into a trust fund? You can bootstrap instead. Don't happen to run into a programming expert who is looking for a co-founder? You will have to search the old-fashioned way, by networking and meeting people.

There can also be a downside to too much early luck. When luck strikes too soon in a business, such as with very early success, you might never develop the thick skin required to take rejection, or the humility to take feedback. You might assume you are a better manager and leader than you really are. You might simply be misled about the timing of your idea, attributing your success instead to another cause. Sometimes success that comes too early can stunt your growth, because you are unable to fulfil it, or to follow up with a subsequent product (similar to musicians whose first single is a huge hit, but who can't follow it up with anything and are forever known as one-hit-wonders).

10

Education and expertise

Education

Education doesn't stop when you get out of school. In fact, it doesn't start when you get into school. Life is learning, from the moment you arrive. Even though he is a voracious reader now, it never suited Ash to go to university. He learned best from reading and doing in a self-directed way.

In a world where all his mates were running off to different universities, gossiping about the latest parties, excited about having new room to roam, he chose less a glamorous option – Staples, a shop selling office supplies.

His former classmates were on holiday with their new girl-friends in between terms. He was helping customers pick out PCs.

They met new friends and went on exciting adventures. Ash studied warranties.

They groaned about long reading assignments. Ash snuck off to the book section to learn just one more thing about the internet and the worldwide web.

Ash dropped out of college twice, repeated some A-levels, tried other diplomas, but it just didn't work out. He didn't go to university, and yet Ash is now by any standards very successful.

Ash is in the minority. Most of the best businesses in the world were founded by people who went to university. For every Richard Branson out there, there are thousands of entre-preneurs who took the traditional route and got their degrees, then went on to create highly successful businesses.

However, correlation is not causation, so does education actually give you an unfair advantage? Does education matter?

The short answer, you won't be surprised to hear, is yes: your education is very important. What doesn't matter so much, however, is how you get that education. We've discussed Intelligence, and now we'll talk about using your intelligence to get educated or develop an Expertise. We'll talk about the education system as a whole, why formal education and post-graduate degrees may or may not be the best path for you, and the different ways to educate yourself and develop expertise.

Education is defined as 'the process of learning, especially at a school or university'.

Having a good Education is a huge Unfair Advantage.

Formal education happens at school or university, while informal education is the education you undertake yourself, of your own volition.

The unfair advantage of a 'good' education

All parents want what's best for their children, and they go to extreme lengths to get it. Top schools and universities are very expensive and incredibly competitive and difficult to get into, and for good reason. According to the 2015 Debrett's 500 list of the most influential people in the UK, including entrepreneurs, more than 40 per cent of them went to fee-paying private schools, even though the sector accounts for only 7 per cent of all schools. This not only confirms the lack of diversity and shows the trend of Britain becoming 'less meritocratic' according to *The Guardian*, it also shows that for whatever reason, going to a private school seems to work to increase the chances of a more prosperous future life.

The number of top entrepreneurs who went to private school is staggeringly high. The list includes Richard Branson (Virgin), Bill Gates (Microsoft), Mark Zuckerberg (Facebook), Elon Musk (Tesla and SpaceX), Jack Dorsey (Twitter and Square), James Dyson (Dyson), Reed Hastings (Netflix), Reid Hoffman (Paypal and LinkedIn), Tony Hseih (Zappos), Kevin Plank (Under Armour), Evan Spiegel (Snapchat), Kevin Systrom (Instagram), Jimmy Wales (Wikipedia), and Nicholas Woodman (GoPro).

Interesting isn't it?

It doesn't seem to bode too well for you if that isn't your background, and doesn't appear to bode well for parents who can't afford expensive fee-paying private schools. And if you look at the data for elite universities, they are all disproportionately filled with students who come from private-school backgrounds, despite continuous efforts by governments to increase social mobility and allow for more underprivileged students at top universities.

However, let's look a little closer and break down the actual benefits of formal education and university degrees. There are three main ones: knowledge, network and signalling.

The first of these benefits is the most obvious purpose of education. Knowledge is what you're taught in schools – which includes literacy, mathematics and facts about the world – and then deeper and generally more specialised subject-specific learning as you get older at university. This gives you the basic tools to engage with the world, from reading to doing simple arithmetic, and it's undeniable that schooling, especially as a child, is crucial to success in life. The more specialised subject areas will give you more in-depth understanding of the world or of a particular field.

The second is network. When you go to university, particularly one that's prestigious and difficult to get into, you will meet others who have also managed to gain entry into that university. The selection process that everyone goes through means that you get a highly curated set of fellow students, who are smart and driven. This is a great source of potential co-founders and business partners. There's also the network to which the university can grant you access if they have good entrepreneurial societies, with professors as potential mentors, and links to investors. The university might even have its own investment fund.

Finally, you have the signalling, which is often referred to as credentialing. It is about showing to others that you have the skills and intelligence for certain jobs. This is the Status and 'personal branding' side of the education system (which is explored Chapter 11). If you go to an elite university, it is a large status booster, and gives you immediate credibility – it's shorthand for 'I'm smart, diligent and talented'. So a top-tier university is by far the most powerful here.

All three of these benefits of education are huge, despite all the criticisms levelled at universities (many of which are valid).

In 2013 venture capitalist Aileen Lee took a hard look at what the fastest-growing unicorn companies (startups which grew to be valued at more than a billion dollars) had in common. These were startups that were less than ten years old. There is much myth and hyperbole surrounding these companies. Aileen wanted to see the data.

Among other observations, she noticed that one 'myth' really did hold to be true: elite universities really do pump out unicorns. Stanford University cranked out the most unicorns, with Harvard, UC Berkeley, and MIT following closely behind. A follow-up study in 2017 by Sage showed the same universities in the same order.

For most entrepreneurs or startup founders, especially non-technical founders who want to raise funding, formal education is an unfair advantage mainly for signalling, status and networking purposes. For non-technical founders, the main value comes from the brand power of having a top university like Harvard, Stanford or MIT, or Cambridge, Oxford or UCL on your LinkedIn and pitchdeck, and from the people you meet there – the network to potentially provide a great co-founder.

Technical unfair advantages

There is, however, one strong context for which what you learn at university, by virtue of the learning itself, is definitely an unfair advantage, and that's specialist technical knowledge.

For example, Google would not have been founded if it wasn't for two Stanford computer science PhD students, Larry Page and Sergey Brin, doing their dissertation in 1996. Originally titled 'BackRub', their dissertation topic (at the encouragement of their supervisor and mentor at the university) was about the structure of the internet and how they could map it out on a graph. This was two nerds just nerding out about this relatively new thing called the internet, without a big vision of become multibillionaires.

The search engine they developed came at a time when there were already plenty of search engines out there, and nobody believed the internet needed another one. However, what drove them to eventually grow Google into one of the most valuable companies in the world was a technical unfair advantage. Larry and Sergey had an Insight that search engines weren't bringing up the best results, and that's because they were just based on keywords. They had another idea, based on the academic citation model, and it simply worked much better. They had the mathematical and computer science education and expertise to be able to apply their creativity to the problem that they'd uncovered, and it worked!

This is a context that shouldn't be overlooked when it comes to formal education and universities. There's a reason why startup hubs develop around university campuses.

This can be true for any field, for example biotech, where biology PhDs apply their education and expertise to a problem. Their unfair advantage is having that knowledge and often being in a strong academic institution that supports and nurtures the startups.

Another example is Demis Hassabis. He could easily be one of those genius case studies we looked at in the Intelligence chapter, since he was a child prodigy at chess, and co-designed and lead-programmed a hugely successful computer game ('Theme Park') at the age of just 17. Deeply educated, with a Double First from Cambridge in computer science, he went on to work on more computer games, this time as lead artificial intelligence (AI) programmer, before founding his own video game development startup. Then it was back to academia for Demis and a PhD in neuroscience at UCL, to find inspiration in the human brain for more AI algorithms.

You can tell someone is freakishly intelligent when simply reading their list of unbelievable accomplishments wears you out. Incredible statistical outliers exist in this world.

Finally, Demis co-founded DeepMind in 2010, a London-based machine learning AI startup with the ambitious mission to 'solve intelligence' and then use intelligence 'to solve everything else'. It certainly paid off financially, as in 2014 Google acquired DeepMind for £400 million. One of Demis's co-founders, Shane Legg, was also an AI PhD. Again, this is where academic institutions prove to be a strong unfair advantage, and not just for signalling and status purposes.

Expertise

Expertise is simple. It is a self-taught process where, for the most part, you learn by doing. Begin by learning enough theory to get you started, but know that ultimately most of the real learning comes when you apply that theory and get feedback from the real world of how it's working. That is how you truly become an expert in something.

Ash found his Unfair Advantage by developing his Expertise, and so did Hasan years later and via a completely different path. Ash did it by reading books after work at Staples, and then immediately applying what he learned to a live project (a shoe eCommerce site), while Hasan did it by taking an online course and then applying the techniques in the real world. Both paths work very well as long as you don't let anything hold you back from applying that knowledge. The goal is to reach the stage of learning-by-doing.

If you don't have the unfair advantage of Money, and are instead living pay cheque to pay cheque, developing your expertise in an in-demand field can be your ticket out. You can freelance on the side, or even use this expertise in your career.

Expertise often means being very good at something quite specific (no one is an 'expert in general') and so that means following your own interests. Formal education and academic institutions are often designed to give you a solid grounding in many different subjects, and won't necessarily help you build your expertise in just one. That's why the emphasis is on you. You can develop expertise without formal education and qualifications: just pick up a book, an audiobook, or an online course, and get started.

Institutions can also be slow-moving, and simply can't keep pace with all the new skills that are in demand by employers. For example, jobs like managing a company's social media didn't exist a decade ago, and with the constantly expanding range of digital skills now in demand, universities are having trouble keeping pace.

As a definition for Expertise, our favourite is the one from Professor Fernand Gobet:

'An expert in a given domain is "somebody who obtains results that are vastly superior to those obtained by the majority of the population".'

This definition can be applied to various domains, from the expert yoga teacher to the superstar tennis player to the expert tax consultant. It also, crucially, doesn't limit you to being an expert in one field. While you probably won't be an expert in *all* fields, you can develop expertise that allows you to deliver to the highest standard in many.

It's easier to become, and be perceived as, an expert at something when there are clear outcomes being delivered, outcomes that are measurable. Both of us have an expertise in SEO. This is measurable as you can see the website at the top of Google search results for the targeted keywords. We both did well by increasing traffic to websites – clearly visible and profitable outcomes, as seen on the search traffic reports and balance sheet. This is something we learned how to do through trial and error, through learning from others and then trying it for ourselves.

In fact, Ash got most of his expertise by tinkering outside of work, on his little side-hustle startups. At a job, putting into action any plan can take many layers of managers and decision-makers, whereas on a side-hustle, you are your own boss and you can simply do it. Ash learned quickly, and the outcome had a direct effect on his pocket.

When we meet people in their early twenties, we always advise them not to pick the job that necessarily pays the most, but the one where they can learn the most. By learning a lot, you get expertise in a specific industry, you acquire specific skills that can be developed further, and you often get some really valuable insights, insights that could turn into startup ideas.

Education can give you the theory and deep knowledge, but the drive to use what you've learnt in real world practical scenarios and being consistent in your learning is vital to becoming a real expert. Not just somebody who knows how to answer questions about a subject but has also done it themselves. As with any form of learning, you've got to commit and continue to develop in order to reach a level where you can get 'results that are vastly superior to those obtained by the majority of the population'.

Education and expertise as your unfair advantage

Are you happy with your level of education? Only you can know if you need to learn more to reach the level you want to be at. We can't change the education we received as children.

But it's never too late to get more education, to improve your learning and your skills. You may decide to do a postgraduate degree, like an MBA or a Masters in Entrepreneurship, or to take an online course like Hasan, or an evening class to up a particular skill such as coding. But how do you decide whether any of it is necessary?

The answer to that question depends on a number of factors, including your other unfair advantages. For example, if you don't yet have a startup idea, there isn't a particular career path you're enjoying or learning a lot from, and you can afford to go back to university, go for it! You may meet someone there, plus if you get into a prestigious university or course you'll give yourself a big status boost and make better connections. You will learn from studying case studies at business school, you could develop deep technical insight by learning something STEM-based, or a gain important critical and cultural skills through studying the humanities. Those with a Masters or PhD may get paid more in future jobs, and in doing so, might be quicker getting to a point where they can quit to start their own company.

Ask yourself:

▶ Do I have the skills to build my company?

▶ Do I know what I am an expert in?

▶ What would I like to be an expert in?

You may already know that you're an expert in something – in which case, you can focus your company on what you're good at, and work on the other skills you need. Even if you feel as if you lack sufficient skills, or expertise, you don't have to wait to start something. Another path if you want to build your 'E' pillar from the MILES Framework is through learning by doing. The ability to keep a 'tinkering' mindset and be a doer more than an intellectual has helped both of us build up our expertise.

If you feel as if you don't yet have an expertise in anything, then you can build it in a variety of ways:

Learning online Ash once met a guy who did some video editing for him and he did an amazing job in 3 hours compared to the full day that others spent on it. Ash asked him how he became a video editing expert and his jokey response was 'I'm YouTube certified'. He meant he'd literally just learned how to do it from free YouTube videos. This is not surprising. It just goes to show that if you have the drive and intention to learn then there are multiple ways to do it. Of course YouTube may not always be the best place to learn, and a structured online course that you invest in could definitely help make things clearer, and will usually reveal more of the insider tips and tricks that people simply don't publish on YouTube for fear of being imitated by competitors.

Books Books can be a great source of information, practical advice and personal wisdom from some of the most successful people in the world. Read as much as you can – or listen to the audiobooks.

Mentors You can't talk to books, however. Speaking to an expert practitioner and asking specific questions will quickly help you increase your knowledge. Meeting potential mentors requires you either to build out your network, or simply pay for their time – one-on-one, or as part of a conference or talk. Sometimes these are free – always try to find out if people you admire are doing events in your area. In our quick start guide we show you other ways of finding a more personal mentor. We'd encourage you to consider mentors who are two to five years ahead of you, as they can teach you the most practical skills. You then need to apply these skills to build expertise. Even if you don't consider them to be mentors, but peers instead, there can be an incredible amount to learn from such people. Be sure to leverage your network to learn from people directly. There's always somebody you know who knows something you don't.

Doing it yourself Finally, and this is the most important advice: do it yourself! Practice. If you can, offer your skills for free, so that you can gain experience. Work for friends and family, people who'll excuse your mistakes. Find other clients, expand your network, get feedback. Work for yourself. Once you're confident in one element, push yourself further, take it to the next level. Another way to solidify expertise is to teach what you know, whether face to face, or by writing up an article or recording a teaching video. It helps you learn it twice.

You don't need to be an expert at everything: that's impossible, so you've got to choose carefully. Go for something that's both in demand and interesting to you. And for areas outside your expertise, lean on others, seek help and double down on the things you have a natural aptitude towards and are happy to spend time learning inside out. You might have Insight but not Expertise in an area – you know the problem really well, but don't have the skills to fix it. That's fine. If you are more inclined to be a generalist than an expert, you may want to find a co-founder with technical expertise in the area for which you have a great idea. That's the point about unfair advantages – no one person will have them all. You can find co-founders or early employees with the expertise that you're missing.

11

Status

'The world more often rewards outward signs of merit than merit itself' La Rochefoucauld

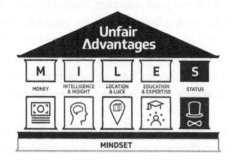

Ash tells the following story about how he once got a job:

I was in the middle of an interview for a brilliant position at a company I really respected. I thought it was going well, and that I was proving myself the perfect candidate. Then the CEO looked at my CV and said, 'I just don't know, Ash.'

'I don't understand', I said. 'What's the problem? Don't I have the credentials?'

'Oh, no, it's not that', he replied, 'in fact, what you've done here is incredibly impressive.'

The problem? He thought I was too young.

In the 22 years I had spent on the planet, I had taught myself how to build websites from scratch. I'd left my home town with nothing but a rucksack and £60 in my pocket. I'd created and sold an eCommerce site which sold shoes all over the world.

Up until this point, all those things were considered ambitious, exceptional, impressive.

Now they seemed meaningless in the face of my being born at the wrong point in time.

It was unfair. How could they toss me away because of my age? How could they look over all my achievements?

I took back my CV. At the top of the page, I looked at the offending line:

Age: 22

With a red pen, I crossed it out, and wrote:

Age: 22 32

'Now do I have the job?' I asked.

Your status is your personal brand. It is how others see you. It is your social standing, your appearance, gender, age, how you dress, stand, talk. It's also your perceived credibility. When Ash was almost denied a job simply because of his young age, that was a concern about his status – whether he could command enough respect, whether he'd have enough perceived wisdom. By crossing out his age, Ash emphasised that it was just a number – and his self-confidence, achievements and experience were what really elevated him as a candidate. He reminded the CEO that status comes from many elements.

High-status people turn heads. People want to meet them. People want to be associated with them. People want to spend time with them.

But it's not just about popularity or celebrity. While in school, status was all about being cool. In adulthood, it's often more about symbols of success, signs of being well educated, and prestigious job titles and occupations. It's about your networks and the way you're seen. Sociologists define it as being about your perceived social value relative to others. In other words, what you can bring to the table.

In addition to this outer status, there's also inner status. Inner status is about how you perceive yourself. It's all about the inner psychology that powerfully boosts your outer status by affecting how you come across, through your confidence and self-esteem.

We'll start by talking about outer status.

Outer status

For better or worse, in most societies, a doctor is perceived as higher in status than a nurse, a CEO higher than an intern, and a billionaire higher than a single mother living on government benefits. And if you're driving a Bentley or Lamborghini, most would consider you higher status than if you were to drive a rusty old car.

Our shared beliefs as a society reflect whom we consider to have higher status – and because of that, the idea of status is riddled with assumptions, prejudices and unconscious biases. This has widespread consequences, beyond just how people are treated on the street. It's why, for example, the unpaid labour of family caregivers, mainly women, is not accounted for on a broader scale in our society.

Status, then, is also about power, as with higher social status comes more prestige, honour and respect, and therefore increased influence.

Higher status commands attention. Higher status makes you an influencer. A high number of social media followers can be a cause and also an effect of high status. However, you can also have high status without any social media followers, simply by being in a culturally prestigious occupation, or working for a high-status brand.

Have you ever noticed that in stories about startup founders, if one of them comes from a high-status company or university, they never fail to mention it? For example, you'll often read: ex-Googler starts a new company. Ex-Goldman Sachs director joins the team. Stanford drop-out founds a new startup. Do you ever wonder why?

There are many ways of increasing your social status, and this chapter is about understanding the power of status, understanding the different forms and contexts of status (unlike what most people talk about, it's not simply about being a privileged 'straight white male', there's a hell of a lot more to it than that – context matters a lot), and finally how to make lemonade with the lemons you've been dealt.

Because remember, status is your *perceived* ability to add value.

Value can be in the form of wisdom, entertainment, spreading good emotions, solving problems for people, achieving something difficult, being cool, trendy, aspirational, attractive or interesting. In this way, it's thankfully more complicated and expansive than just whether you're 'upper class', 'white' or 'male' – we all have a certain status in different situations.

As entrepreneurs or aspiring entrepreneurs, to some extent or another, our 'why' or motivation for starting is usually tied to increasing our status. Not always the most mentally healthy of motivations, but the reality is that most of us strive for success to achieve some kind of significance, to feel important.

Status can be in the form of titles, ranks or qualifications, like *Sir* Richard Branson or *Lord* Alan Sugar, it can be in the form of prestigious universities or companies, it could be about being male, being upper class, being tall, being white (or being fair-skinned), being beautiful (whatever society deems beauty to be), displaying wealth, being a native English speaker, having a particular accent, wearing the right kind of watch, driving the right kind of car, being famous, having friends in high places, or even just signalling that you're part of the right subculture or are cool.

All these are social signals that most people unconsciously look for and react to. As hierarchical creatures, we as human beings, just like other social animals, are always trying to figure out where we fit on the totem pole (on the social hierarchy).

For example, in most cultures, an older age is indicative of experience and wisdom, and therefore warrants respect. Even in the West, being older is mostly a good thing and can be considered a sign of higher status for getting jobs, hence Ash's experience at the beginning of this chapter. In tech startup culture, however, being young seems to be more respected, as you're more likely to be hip to the newest trends.

Prominent sociologist Pierre Bourdieu explains status as being comprised of three different types of capital: economic, cultural and social.

Economic Capital is covered under the Money chapter in this section and is simply the concrete and tangible form of wealth in the sense of money, assets and property.

Cultural Capital is linked to your social class (or even your subculture), which is reflected in your accent, credentials, set of tastes, hobbies and pastimes, manner of speech, manner of dress, posture, possessions, etc.

As an example, a 2016 study by the Social Mobility Commission found that graduates who wear brown shoes to their interviews are missing out on top investment banking jobs in the City. This wouldn't come as a shock to anyone familiar with the banking industry. But why? Why is such a silly thing like wearing brown shoes instead of black an issue? Snobbery, that's why. Employers use unspoken dress codes that, when broken, are tell-tale signs that the applicant is from a less privileged social background, i.e. from a lower class. The *Evening Standard* reported: 'Bright working class candidates are often rejected for jobs as they are unaware of the "opaque" dress codes that richer children grow up with, experts found.'

This sort of thing is rife. It's a prime example of elitism at play, with firms going way beyond merit to figure out 'culture fit', and thereby keeping opportunities mainly to the upper classes in society. The report added: 'A candidate from a non-privileged background was told at one bank that while he was "clearly quite sharp", he was "not quite the right fit" and that his tie was "too loud".' The report also highlighted that banks mostly hire from a just a handful of elite universities, like Oxford, Cambridge and the London School of Economics.

Social Capital, the third form of Status, is your **Network**, your relationships, your connections. We include this in Status because who you know is part of your status (which is why people often like to name-drop a high-status person in conversation, like a celebrity, for example, to increase their own status by association). Your Network is the people you're connected with in some way and who therefore could open doors for you to opportunities, give you valuable insights and information, and act as allies and potential collaborators. The way to increase your connections – your network – is through adding value, finding commonalities and being social. Your network is who would return your call, reply to your email or take a coffee meeting with you.

The interesting thing about Status? All the other pillars of the MILES Framework help increase Status as well. As social animals, status affects, and is affected by, virtually everything we do.

Ash grew up in Birmingham, dropped out of school and

didn't go to university, and his parents, as first-generation immigrants, didn't know anyone in the tech industry to give him mentorship or a leg-up. He was pretty low on social, economic and cultural capital at the start of his journey. The primary way that Ash was able to increase his Status was through building up his Expertise in digital marketing and growth strategies. And that's how he ended up being the first marketing director at Just Eat.

You can even have higher Status simply by virtue of your Location. Successful entrepreneur and investor, James Caan, of *Dragon's Den* fame, purposely used a Mayfair address for his business when he was starting out to suggest that he already had success wealth, and worked in an area with other rich and influential people.

When travelling to other cities or other parts of the world, we feel the Status that we get simply by virtue of being from London.

The Collison brothers (see Chapter 8) were evidently very Intelligent from a young age, but through taking up places at Harvard and MIT – even if they later dropped out – they added prestigious institutions to their CVs and increased their social networks. And so, their Education, and also their existing achievements in a previous startup they founded, increased their Status.

Likewise, Money obviously increases your Status in society, through economic power (just look at Trump, for instance). It tends to be *displays* of wealth that make people react differently to you. Ash experienced this first hand when he made enough money to get a Porsche. People certainly reacted differently to him. Ash didn't like it and made sure his next car was less flashy.

(Flashiness, by the way, has different value in different social contexts and cultures, so it's definitely not always a good thing, with most high-status people actively attempting to downplay their displays of wealth, such as the upper classes in Britain.)

Prejudice and unconscious bias

Because it's so tied up with how others perceive you, and how you view others, the unfortunate reality of Status is that it can be very linked to conscious and unconscious bias and prejudice. Sometimes people will have preconceptions about you based purely on your skin colour, ethnicity, gender, age, accent, religion, sexuality, name, and the class and subculture signals that you give off. This comes from the unfortunate reality of prejudice and biased pattern recognition.

The truth is, if you look and sound like a middle-to-upper class young, white, nerdy hacker guy, and then they find out you've dropped out of Harvard, you're more likely to get investment for your startup idea. You've got a higher chance of success in raising funds. You've got a higher chance of success in finding a co-founder. You have a higher chance of success in attracting a strong team.

This is where pattern recognition can seem unfair.

Having those characteristics doesn't guarantee success by any means. It's definitely not the be-all-and-end-all. However, there's no denying that they help.

If you're thinking you don't have this unfair advantage, you don't fit that mould – there's good news. By being an 'outsider', in any form, you get powerful Insights that can be missed by those who are the typical young men who usually become founders. In other words, status is also a double-edged sword, just like every other unfair advantage.

This is the same reason why diversity and inclusion are starting to be recognised as valuable in terms of a company's bottom line, because having a variety of perspectives and people from different societal subcultures helps. Diversity isn't simply about race or gender, although these are important. It is also about a multitude of other factors, whether it be different ethnicities, religions, sexual orientations or political leanings.

Difference gives you Insights. And as we've discussed, Insight is a very powerful Unfair Advantage.

You saw it from Tristan Walker's example and his multi-blade razors. He was able to find an unmet need simply by being African American and realising an obvious truth.

Another example is Sara Blakely, founder of Spanx. Being a woman helped her uncover a real need, and have a unique Insight. This is her story:

Sara Blakely – using your outsider status

Spanx is a billion dollar 'shapewear' company founded by Sara Blakely, who's now a billionaire. Hers is an incredible story of grit, determination, and of course some luck as well.

Sara was the daughter of a lawyer and brought up in a middle-class household in Florida. She was a communications graduate from Florida State University who aspired to be a lawyer too.

However, she had a few early failures. First she couldn't pass the LSAT examination, despite attempting it twice. She then lowered her sights and tried to get the role of Goofy at Walt Disney World, but failed at that as well because she wasn't tall enough. Next, she even tried her hand at one of the most terrifying things for most people: stand-up comedy. Again, it didn't work out.

She ended up in sales, selling fax machines door-to-door. This job was absolutely brutal. She spent seven years being rejected almost daily. People would hang up on her cold calls and rip up her business card in front of her.

The plus side? She developed a tough skin, and an ability to turn 'no's into 'yes's as a job. This came in really handy for her.

'It was great life training', Blakely says. 'I had to learn to be concise, to tell them what's in it for them.'

Unfulfilled by her job, she wanted something more.

One day she pulled over to the side of the road in her car and had a 'rock-bottom' moment. She couldn't take the rejection and people slamming doors in her face anymore. She decided to quit.

'And so, I went home that night and I wrote down in my journal: "I want to invent a product that I can sell to millions of people that will make them feel good." This was something that I set intention for, I had really asked the universe to give me an idea that I could bring to the world.'

She literally had this vision. She was set on having an amazing big idea, one that could possibly get her on Oprah.

In fact, that was her first vision and dream for herself back when she was in college, to get on the *Oprah Winfrey Show* and sit on her sofa. She had no idea how she was going to do it but that was what she wanted. At first, she thought she'd get there through taking on a famous case as a lawyer, then she thought stand-up comedy would get her sitting on Oprah's couch.

But during her time as a salesperson, she had an insight. She was forced to wear tights in the Florida heat for her job and she hated the seamed foot, but liked how the top of the tights would compress and create a firmer silhouette with no pantyline. She had an 'aha' moment one day when she cut off the feet to go to a party, and although they rolled up her leg under her trousers, they gave her the result she wanted.

This was her 'Eureka!' moment. This would lead to a product that millions of women would want. And that's how it all started, with this Insight, one that a man would never have had because it was so specific to the experience of women.

She researched patents herself and got one for her design,

and then she bootstrapped her way to success with her sales skills, drive, grit, and the $5,000 she had in savings.

Once she had invented her product, she sent out a gift basket to none other than Oprah. And luckily for her, Oprah loved it and recommended it to everyone. Her dream was realised.

This stroke of luck accelerated her growth massively, and it was the hustle and drive she put into her business that got her there.

She bootstrapped (didn't raise funding), she admits, because she actually did not even know you could raise so much money from investors – she was unaware of it as an option. Luckily for her, she succeeded and owns 100 per cent of her business, which is very rare for a business that becomes so large.

So as you can see, Sara Blakely used what many would consider to be a possible disadvantage (being a female founder) into an advantage, by leveraging a unique insight she could only have had as a woman, similar to Tristan Walker.

By having the status of being some type of minority, whether that's an ethnic minority, or coming from a white working-class background with a strong regional accent, or even being a woman (which obviously isn't a minority at all in the population, but still is as a startup founder), you can actually work things in your favour. Your status is a double-edged sword in that it enables you to stand out more, and therefore be more memorable.

Ultimately it comes down to focusing on making the business work. Maybe you need more traction and customers to raise funding from investors if you don't fit the typical mould of who they invest in – that's not always a bad thing. Maybe you'll end up making a bootstrapped startup that makes profit early on. These are all possibilities.

So as we said before, it's not about focusing on the

negatives, or letting those get to you, it's more about knowing the realities – that it's not necessarily a level playing field – and taking action regardless to maximise your chances. If that means changing your strategy, then do it.

Let's remind ourselves as well that there may be some investors or VCs who are so eager to improve their diversity that you actually end up with a better chance! There has been progress in mindsets and unconscious biases, and it's important to bear that in mind as well.

The uses of cultural capital

If you wore formal business attire to your meeting with the bank to get a bank loan, it might increase your chances of getting one.

If you wore the same clothes in Silicon Valley, you'd probably be less likely to get investment.

Similarly, being only 20 years old is going to decrease your chances at the bank, and increase your chances in the Valley.

Why?

Because each has a different subculture.

What's high status and a symbol of seriousness at your traditional bank is try-hard and borderline laughable in the young, casual California culture of tech startups.

This is also about signalling, because you signal your membership to a subculture or class by how you dress, speak and behave.

Being in the same subculture or class helps you to build relationships, because you will probably have a shared commonality. Similar tastes in music and fashion, similar interests and hobbies.

You'll later read about Melanie Perkins, co-founder of Canva. One of the things she was learn to kitesurf, even though she hated it, just to be able to impress a potential investor, and to attend his kitesurfing investor event. It worked.

Bestselling business author Seth Godin refers to this phenomenon as the basis of all marketing. He calls it 'People like us do things like this'. If you can leverage that tribal aspect of the human brain, you can influence a lot of people.

Those tribal instincts start young. Remember the Collison brothers who founded their first startup before they left school, and became billionaires in their early twenties? Yes, they were Intelligent, yes, they had crucial Insight. But they also had a form of cultural capital that helped a little. Status is about how we sit in the world, what position our parents occupy, and how we view the possibilities available to us. The Collison brothers were born into a family of entrepreneurs.

Patrick says this about the fact that his parents were scientists-turned-entrepreneurs:

'Entrepreneur is a long, fancy French word, but it didn't seem like something you aspire to … It seemed normal, because whatever your parents do seems normal.'

This is exactly it. If you grow up surrounded by adults who are entrepreneurs, then you will assume it's normal to be an entrepreneur. More than that – you'll know what an entrepreneur is. This is the sort of intangible unfair advantage that is sometimes hard to see – the privilege of possibility. If you grow up in a home where your parents aren't entrepreneurs, and don't know any, it can be a harder career option to imagine.

It's something that Tristan Walker would have been familiar with, and which changed when he went to boarding school. 'I got to see how the other half lived', Walker says. 'I went to school with Rockefellers and Fords, I got to understand the power of a last name.' He learned the power of status, but also the possibilities that existed. More than that, he learned how to behave in that world, expand his networks and use those links. The average class size at this school was just fourteen students. They had amazing state-of-the-art technology, the best teachers and facilities. He describes how the mostly white economically elite environment of his boarding school taught him to 'weave in and out of different social group types'. 'It completely changed my life', he later said.

In these two examples, we can see how cultural capital in the form of knowledge can be passed down from parents to children. Tristan Walker didn't even 'know' about the opportunities of Silicon Valley, but some kids like the Collisons grow up hearing all about it and were encouraged in that direction.

Family can help us increase our status in other ways. Sara Blakely says her father used to ask them at dinnertime every day what they had failed at that day. And he wasn't happy until they had something to tell him every day. This taught them not to fear failure, which Sara attributes to helping her succeed.

Richard Branson recounts his mother teaching her children self-reliance from a really young age, in a way that is shocking to most of us nowadays. In a particularly extreme instance, he was around six years old and acting up in the car, so as punishment and about 4 miles away from his grandma's house, she kicked him out of the car and told him to find his own way there.

Status even applies to startups as well. Before Ash headed up Just Eat's first TV ad campaign, which was only made after they got their funding of £10.5 million from VCs in 2009, part of Ash's responsibility as marketing director was to create brand partnership deals. While they were doing well in both their restaurant and customer growth, the partnership deals weren't getting much traction. The brands would drag their feet, and just generally didn't show much enthusiasm in partnering up with this 'online food ordering' startup. After that first TV ad, an expensive primetime slot during X Factor, it was a different story. Suddenly everyone started returning Ash's calls. Suddenly they all wanted to partner up. Which just shows that status works for a brand as well, and a big TV ad campaign gave Just Eat status and broadcast the fact that they weren't just a scrappy startup anymore.

One of these partner companies was Virgin, and Ash was invited to meet Richard Branson. The fact that Ash had met one of the most famous billionaire entrepreneurs in the world meant that his own status suddenly increased. This was a form of social capital. Who you know, and are associated with, has a really strong impact on people's unconscious biases.

Your network

'*Who* you know is more important than *what* you know.'

Anon

Building your network is all about your proactiveness in forming and maintaining mutually beneficial relationships.

The key phrase in that formula is 'mutually beneficial relationships'.

And to make it easier for you, you need to learn to present and package your status more effectively. This is often referred to as 'personal branding'.

Beware, though, there are many pitfalls which can make you come across as smarmy, insufferable and manipulative. Proceed with caution when it comes to any status games.

With a large and strong network, you gain more powerful relationships, which can always allow you to get more opportunities, more relevant information and insights, find a co-founder, an investor, or get introduced to people who can help you to start, grow and even exit a startup if that's what you wish to do.

A large and powerful network can give you mentors, investors, peers, and customers. Practical advice on how to increase your Network is in Part Three of the book.

Inner status

Your Inner Status is an extremely powerful way to increase your Outer Status. It is your self-esteem. Your confidence. Self-esteem is just a fancy way of saying 'liking yourself'. And whether or not you're confident or have high self-esteem always shines through to other people. They pick up on it, consciously and unconsciously, through your body language, voice tonality and other subtle clues in your behaviour. That's how inner status increases your outer status.

If you like and value yourself, you will have high self-esteem. You'll come across as confident, competent, likeable, trustworthy and engaging.

And if you don't, you need to work on liking and valuing yourself.

The objection we usually hear to this is: I haven't yet achieved much, how can I like myself? I'm unhappy with where I am in life, I am lazy, I procrastinate, I have trouble staying motivated, I indulge in self-defeating and self-sabotaging behaviour.

Well, you know what? We all do.

That's the dirty secret. Hardly anybody, except possibly a handful of outliers in the world, fails to experience these things.

You don't need to be perfect to succeed. That's the thing to bear in mind.

In his book *Atomic Habits*, James Clear outlines how you can take the baby steps necessary to change your life by implementing new habits incrementally and patiently.

That's the self-improvement side.

Get clear on your goals and values. What do you want for your lifestyle? What do you want for your legacy? What moral code are you willing to stick to?

Then once you're clear on that, simply take the baby steps

to getting there while focusing on why you're doing it.

For now, however, know that you need a balance of self-belief and self-improvement, and you also need to (almost paradoxically) know the limits of possibility for yourself in the short term. We overestimate what we can achieve in a month, and dramatically underestimate what we can achieve in a decade. Be sure to love yourself for where you're at in life at this moment.

If you feel you're unlovable for some sin or vice or some other reason, just love yourself for being self-aware about it and then being willing to change it.

You'll have setbacks, but as long as you persevere in improving your self-discipline and your focus, you'll get there step-by-step.

(And if you feel you may have completely irrational beliefs or psychological patterns that are destructive and may come from something in childhood, then please feel free to get some help! The great thing is that nowadays there's more help for mental health issues and it's quickly becoming less stigmatised.)

If you pin your self-love and happiness to something external, you'll either keep moving the finish line and never be happy, or you'll experience the most profound anti-climax in your life and get depressed when you realise that achieving your external goal does not fill the inner void.

Imposter syndrome

Sometimes I hear about how 'all creators feel like a fraud sometimes' and I'm like, 'Oh god, I never feel like a fraud … am I truly a creator?' And then I'm like, 'Oh, never mind! I'm good!'

Hank Green, entrepreneur, educator and author

'I'm out of my depth.'

'I don't belong here.'

'I'm gonna be found out.'

Have these thoughts ever run through your head?

To some extent, we all experience this.

It's a phenomenon known as Imposter Syndrome. You may feel as if you're an imposter, or a fraud, and that the position, achievements or praise you got were completely unearned.

Self-doubt is normal. One 2007 study in the *Chronicle of Higher Education* estimates that up to 70 per cent of people might experience it at least once in their lives.

And we can say that if you're about to pursue a tough path like entrepreneurship, your chances of experiencing it are probably even higher. Completely normal. It's so incredibly common. Don't compare your behind-the-scenes to everyone else's highlight reel.

The truth is, nobody really knows the right thing to do in every situation, and even huge success stories have a lot of missteps and failures.

You can't see into other people's heads, only into your own. This gives you the impression that everybody else knows what they're doing and you're the only one that doesn't.

Belief that you don't have the competence or merit to be where you are can be part of this feeling. You need to have faith in your ability to step into a role and learn to make it work, and simply pushing yourself slightly outside your comfort zone more regularly will help you build that confidence.

Kylie Jenner – stepping beyond inherited status

Hate them or love them, undeniably the Kardashian-Jenner clan have somehow, against all odds, managed to extend their 15 minutes of fame into over 15 years. Famous for being famous, and criticised constantly by almost every pundit, they must be doing something 'right' in the business sense to keep the enormous attention and influence that they yield.

Wearing a smart black double-breasted blazer and gracing the cover of *Forbes* August 2018 issue, a familiar dark-haired, pouty-lipped young woman was described as '$900 million cosmetics queen Kylie Jenner. At 21, she's set to be the youngest ever self-made billionaire'.

Watch out Evan Spiegel!

Watch out Collison brothers!

Watch out Mark Zuckerberg, who had held the record for youngest person to hit self-made billionaire status, aged 23.

By March 2019, Forbes confirmed that Kylie had indeed become a 'self-made' billionaire at 21.

She is by far the richest Kardashian-Jenner at the moment. A monumental achievement (especially to overtake Kim!). But some people on the internet had an issue with this Forbes cover.

Out came a tweet from Dictionary.com: 'Self-made means having succeeded in life unaided.' They went on: 'Used in a sentence: *Forbes* says that Kylie Jenner is a self-made woman.'

For a bit of background, Kylie has appeared in the hugely successful reality TV show *Keeping Up With The Kardashians* since she was ten years old. Being mainstays of popular culture and dominating on television, the tabloids, and then on social media, the Kardashian-Jenners have leveraged Kim Kardashian West's fame in one way or another. Kim's two Kardashian sisters have become celebrities in their own right, with a string of their own businesses and projects, from clothing to makeup lines to boutiques, with their mum embracing her role as their manager, taking her cut of all their businesses. Then the younger two half-sisters of Kim Ð the Jenners, Kendall and Kylie Ð got in on the act.

First, Kendall and Kylie were lumped together in the public

consciousness, but slowly, as they got older, Kendall became a fully-fledged supermodel. Kylie was slightly left behind, lacking the slender and tall body type that tends to be chosen by the mainstream modelling industry. Instead, she was more interested in business.

She threw her energies into social media and became the social media star of her generation, the generation after the millennials, Generation Z. She was in a prime position to take advantage of a social network that was popular with this age group Ð Snapchat.

She loved it, and grew one of the largest Snapchat followings in the world.

In terms of Status, being in a hit reality show that defined a pop-culture generation meant that she was one of the most famous faces in the world. And when it comes to her environment, the cultural capital that she had growing up in the Kardashian-Jenner clan was astounding, with their mother as their manager, and their amazing talent for attracting and maintaining attention, and monetising that with an army of companies that are desperate to partner with them, or use them to access their huge fanbase.

In terms of Money, she had a mind-blowing level of income, reportedly having been paid half a million dollars per episode she appeared in (and she has appeared in over 150, which means from the show alone she has made over $75 million). She is paid roughly a million dollars for each of her social media sponsored posts. She has fashion lines, and endorsement deals that pay her millions as well. She could take on any business endeavour she wanted without ever risking her wealth in any way, shape or form.

In terms of Inner Status, Kylie definitely had confidence after years in the limelight, but she did have one hang-up. Reportedly, she was teased at school for her lips. Compared to her Kardashian sisters, her lips were much thinner.

This insecurity lead to her having lip fillers done when she was only 15 years old.

This helped drive the trend for big lips even further, with teen girls (and some boys) doing things like the Kylie lip challenge where they'd use suction from a drinking glass to puff up their lips. This is the level of status and influence that Kylie had as a 15-year-old.

She also started a trend, even before the lip fillers, of using makeup to make the lips seem larger. Noticing that others were following her example, Kylie, and probably an army of managers and business advisers as well, came up with the idea of selling 'Kylie Lip Kits' in 2015. They partnered with a very experienced 'white-label' cosmetics company and did an initial run of 15,000 'lip kits'. Kylie invested $250,000 of her own money to get it developed.

She then promoted it to her millions of social media fans diligently in the run-up to the launch. It is reported that they sold out of all 15,000 kits within 1 minute.

They rebranded to Kylie Cosmetics, relaunched in early 2016, and sold $19 million worth of product within 24 hours. Kylie used an online eCommerce platform to take care of the sales and fulfilment. The rest of the multimillion-dollar business is handled by just twelve staff, only seven of whom are full time.

Her vision was strong though. Back in 2015, before the launch of her lip kits, she mused to *Interview*:

'If I could do whatever I wanted, I would have a successful makeup line, and I would want to hopefully start more businesses, and just be, like, a businesswoman.' This was weeks before people had even heard of a lip kit.

After launching her namesake makeup company, Kylie Cosmetics, Kylie has used her loyal fanbase and powerful social media platform to catapult the brand into one of the fastest-growing companies in the beauty business. Forbes reports that Kylie Cosmetics has sold more than $630 million's worth of makeup since its initial launch, which includes an estimated $330 million in 2017 alone. Combining all of its profits, Forbes estimates that the brand alone is worth nearly $800 million, of which Kylie maintains sole ownership – it's a fully bootstrapped business (and that's not even all of her earnings: She also rakes in product endorsements, cashes in her *Keeping Up with the Kardashians* pay cheques, and boasts a Kendall + Kylie clothing line and a Puma deal).

Jenner credits her more than 100 million social media followers as the key to her success.

'Social media is an amazing platform', she says. 'I have such easy access to my fans and my customers.'

So you can see how strong Kylie's unfair advantages were, and it's interesting to compare her story with Huda Kattan's from a few chapters ago, who also started her own wildly successful cosmetics startup, and how those unfair advantages differed.

Status as your unfair advantage

So what should you do about Status?

You should at least have some sense of whether or not you have high social status. You know your own background and the privileges – or lack thereof – that you've experienced. But because of the deeply social aspect to this particular unfair advantage, and the value placed on certain types of privilege, we can often lie to ourselves, or not see it clearly. This is an example of where asking friends and colleagues to be honest with you can really help.

If you do have a form of status, be sure to highlight it *when necessary*. This means that if you have an impressive university or job at a famous company in your history, make sure it's there on your CV. Don't downplay those kinds of achievements.

But if you want to stay likeable and keep your friends, you should probably refrain from highlighting or trying to big up your status too often. Bragging is one way to immediately lower your status. Status is more nuanced than shouting from the rooftops. There's a place for humility, and different cultures and subcultures are variably tolerant of self-aggrandising.

If you're naturally humble, speak up about your achievements, and if you're speaking up too much when it's not necessary, pipe down about it, because if you do have an ace up your sleeve in terms of accomplishments, you'll have even higher status in people's eyes when they find out about it anyway.

If you feel that you don't fit the mould of a typically higher-status individual, don't despair. Be aware of the prejudices you might face, educate yourself on the cultural codes of places you want to join, and, most importantly, remember that everything you are (not just your family background) contributes to the value you can bring: your personality, your mindset, your education, insight and location.

And don't forget the importance of Inner Status. Your confidence and self-esteem will shine through. Make sure to work on liking yourself, and building your conviction in yourself. Bear in mind that everyone feels unconfident or out of their depth sometimes. Everyone gets imposter syndrome. You have to push through it. Question your inner critic. Push yourself outside of your comfort zone regularly, so you can start having faith in yourself that you'll manage. Get that feeling of resourcefulness inside you.

In fact, for Status, it's most important to develop your Inner Status (your confidence and self-esteem) first, rather than your Network or your Expertise. The latter two determine what role you will play in your startup – Networking is better for the commercial co-founder, and Expertise more important for the technical partner. But both partners need self-confidence to succeed. Then combined you will make a strong management team – what all investors are looking for.

Always keep in mind how others succeed and what status they may have had before they started. Don't feel disempowered by others' success, there's always more to it than meets the eye.

Status as a double-edged sword

A lack of status can be the impetus to drive you to make something of yourself. Just think of Oprah Winfrey, Sarah Blakely, or Richard Branson walking 4 miles home. Entrepreneurs who are stripped of any advantage simply because of who they are or who their parents are often use this lack of recognition to drive their internal motivation and confidence.

What can happen when you have too much status? Simple: you can become blinded to reality, or lose touch with what life is like for the average person.

PART THREE

THE STARTUP
QUICK-START GUIDE

12

The why

'Quit your job, and start a business! Be your own boss! Be an entrepreneur!'

These are the kinds of things you'll hear to encourage you to start your own startup.

What they fail to mention, however, is how damn hard it is.

In the social media era we now live in, you only see the rosy side of the story. People hide their failures and hide the difficulty of being their own boss.

There's a benefit to being an employee. You get a set structure – you get at least *some* predictability and stability.

However, the fact you're reading this book tells us that you're probably one of us, the crazy ones who actually want to go through with it and give it a shot, despite the risk of failure, despite the risk of loss of income, despite the difficulty, stress, and sheer graft you'll have to put in to make it happen.

You've learned that startup success, just like any meaningful success in life, is a mixture of both hard work and luck. You've learned that we're far from having a level playing field, far from having a pure meritocracy. Just as life is unfair, so is business, and some people have a head-start when it comes to starting and growing their own startup. You've also learned that, despite the un-level playing field, we all have unfair advantages, and that even what can seem like a disadvantage can actually be turned into an advantage by having the right mindset. You've learned that mindset, personality, money, intelligence and insight, location and luck (right place, right time), education and expertise, and status all play *massive* roles in setting you up for success in work and startups. You've also learned that you can utilise mental models that are empowering, but still realistic, avoiding the most egregious feelings of failure and instead realising that nobody has 100 per cent control of the outcomes in their life.

Now, in Part Three of this book, we will guide you through the practical steps of how to launch your own startup, and maximise your chances of success. We'll begin with the most important question: your 'why'.

The question that people most commonly fail to answer properly is 'why'. Why start a startup? Why take this arduous path into the unknown? Why not just stick to the tried-and-tested, much more predictable path of being an employee?

You'd think that as entrepreneurs writing about entrepreneurship, we'd be unequivocally encouraging about starting your own business.

However, we believe that just as medicine is becoming more and more personalised and bespoke to each person's unique DNA, so too must advice become less of a one-size-fits-all and more about your unique personality and circumstances. And that's what we did in Part Two, helped guide you through identifying and analysing your personality, mindset and unique set of circumstantial assets – your MILES.

If, for example, your personality is naturally *very* high in neuroticism, in other words you are the type to experience a lot of anxiety, launching a startup *may* not be the path for you. There are no hard and fast rules, just signposts of what might work better for you. Every personality trait has both strengths and weaknesses, and you may be great at anticipating potential problems and could be a fantastic second-in-command at a startup, such as a co-founder who joins the leading founder a little later, or as an early employee.

You have to ask yourself why you're launching a startup, or why you're choosing any path to pursue. What are you trying to gain and achieve, and what are you trying to avoid? That's how motivation works – it's the proverbial carrot and stick. A carrot is dangled in front of a donkey to keep it moving forward because it wants to eat the carrot, and the stick keeps it moving forward through the pain of being hit with a stick. The carrot is the reward that you are striving towards, and the stick is the pain you are avoiding. As sophisticated as we think we are as human beings, this way of thinking about motivation is surprisingly accurate.

Psychology tells us that for most people, the away-from motivation (the stick) is actually the more powerful motivator.

Ash was motivated by seeing his parents working hard and struggling with a very limited pay packet from a simple factory job. He didn't want that life for himself. He wanted less scarcity for his own life. He didn't like how constrained his parents were financially, and how that limited their choices when it came to what they could afford, and the freedom they had. He was also eager to prove to his family and friends that he could succeed despite not going to university. Finally, he also did it to pursue his ideas. He was called a maverick as an employee, as he never just sat there and followed the rules – he always had creative, outside-the-box ideas which he wanted to pursue.

Overall, Ash was more motivated by escaping the limited lifestyle that he grew up with than attracted by status symbols like a Rolex and a Ferrari. Later on, Ash's 'why' became more about giving back, about giving more underprivileged people the opportunity that he had. That social impact mission became his primary driver.

For Hasan, it was the motivation of not having a boss, of having the freedom and flexibility of working whenever and from wherever he wanted. Hasan wanted to be able to work on stuff that he cared about and got fulfilment from. He wanted to teach more people about the freedom and adventure that entrepreneurship gives you, and the positive social impact that this can create, persuading people that they don't have to stay in unfulfilling jobs that don't make the best use of their talents and passions.

For you, maybe it's something similar. Or maybe you want to have the fame, the fortune, the glitz and glamour, and the flashiness and the luxury. Or maybe you want to help society. Maybe you want to save the environment. Whatever your motivation is, there is no right or wrong answer.

We all have a higher self and a lower self, and the best way to align your motivations fully is if there's something in it for you for your 'lower self' (trying to live a certain lifestyle, getting the recognition, the money, the status, the freedom), and for your 'higher self', which is hopefully much bigger in scope (helping others, spreading opportunity, pulling people out of poverty, saving lives, saving the environment, giving people access to a good education).

And while we mentioned that there's no right or wrong 'why', be aware that if you're only seeking status and recognition from others, if you get it, you probably still won't be happy. Success for the approval of others is inevitably hollow. There needs to also be a bigger intrinsic motivation for true happiness and fulfilment to come.

That's why you need to **define success for yourself**. If you do not, Hollywood, the media, friends, family, colleagues, not to mention social media, will define it for you. You will see what looks like success, and you'll chase it. Then, the goalposts will keep moving and you'll never feel that you're happy. If you can define success for yourself, and make that definition less focused on external measures (like getting to a certain net worth, or being able to afford to fly first class everywhere you go) but more on internal and higher-level needs (helping others, putting a 'ding' in the universe with your impact – like Steve Jobs), then that's something you will have the power to achieve. Make your criteria for success process based rather than outcome based. You can't control the outcome because luck always plays a role, but you can control your own actions and processes to do the right thing in alignment with your values and goals.

Beware of confusing society's *symbols* of success (fast cars, private jets, designer clothes, fancy restaurants, exotic holidays) and *actual* success (happiness, fulfilment, self-actualisation, growth, learning, adding value to others, having positive impact, having the freedom to spend quality time with the people you love).

This is easier said than done, but as long as you think about it and bear it in mind, you'll be inoculated against the worst of the negative emotions and cognitive dissonance of not getting to where you envisage, or getting there and realising you're still not happy.

Now that those thoughts about true success and happiness are planted in the back of your mind, let's move on from the philosophical to the practical. The next few chapters will teach you the practical steps required to stack the odds in your favour to succeed in your startup. Even if you decide to become an early employee at a startup instead, the advice that follows is still very valuable knowledge, as it will let you know which startup to join. Just like Ash, you're unlikely to be paid a high salary, but you'll be able to get shares, and those startup shares are only worth something if the startup doesn't fall flat on its face (which is where most early-stage startups end up).

You can also use this advice as your criteria to assess which startup to work for, or even which startup to invest in (if you're blessed with the Unfair Advantage of Money). This, in concert with the MILES assessment which analyses the unfair advantages you have (and can use to analyse the unfair advantages that the founders have), allows you to maximise your chances of success, and of the success of the startup you choose.

Finally, the type of startup you choose is going to have massive consequences on not just your chances of success (based on your unfair advantages) but also on your lifestyle. That's why we discuss the two broad types of startups in the next chapter: Lifestyle Startups and Hyper-Growth Startups.

For example, as the founder of a hyper-growth startup, you can pretty much say goodbye to any notion of work–life balance, having a social life, having hobbies, or anything like that. Your life is going to be your startup, and that's pretty much it.

Lifestyle startups are still intense, but not as intense as hyper-growth startups. They're also not as binary in terms of huge success or total failure. They're more likely to succeed, not likely to need funding, and even less likely to make you *extremely* wealthy.

Your 'why' (your goals) and your unfair advantages will help determine the type of startup you should aim for.

The type of startup

Lifestyle startups

Lifestyle startups (or lifestyle businesses) are so called because they are designed to sustain a certain lifestyle. That could be a certain income, a certain work schedule, or it could be that there's a constraint placed on their growth – whether by the founders' design or by the local or niche nature of their market. Lifestyle startups usually don't need external investors.

For example, professional service businesses like accountancy firms, law firms, marketing agencies and consultancies usually stay small. This is because to service more clients, you need more staff. So the only way to really scale it is to hire more people. This is expensive. Also, these startups usually service clients locally in a traditional face-to-face way.

Another example might be a startup selling equipment online for a sport that's very niche. So only the 10,000 people who play that sport or are interested in it are in the total addressable market. It will be a lifestyle business.

Or how about a fitness coach who garners a bit of a social media following, and decides to do her own brand of clothes and protein shakes? That's likely to a be a lifestyle business, because a single person, unless they become a giant mainstream celebrity, is not likely to have a big enough reach to get to the size of needing to operate like a hyper-growth Silicon-Valley-style tech startup.

The term 'lifestyle business' is often used pejoratively by people in the startup world, and you can invariably sense a certain level of condescension. This is because investors are not interested in investing in lifestyle businesses; they make their money from the big, bold 'moonshot' ideas – the ones which aim to disrupt a whole industry and become a unicorn (worth over a billion dollars) like Airbnb, Just Eat, and Revolut. That's their business model in the VC world: invest in loads of startups with potential for hyper-growth and hope that one or two make it really big, while the others fail. For example, Marc Andreesen, co-founder of the legendary Andreesen Horowitz VC firm, explained how they invest in around 200 startups a year, and that around 15 of those 200 (7.5 per cent) will generate 95 per cent of all economic returns. In other words, just a handful of hyper-growth startups become successes and the rest flounder. This is the binary nature of hyper-growth startups – it's either succeed big, or fail completely.

Lifestyle startups, by contrast, are not binary and are more conventional. By 'not binary' we mean they're not either a one or a zero, a hit or a miss. They don't have such a strong dichotomy of succeed or fail but are more nuanced. You can succeed, make a profit, but you can also make less money than if you were still an employee, for example. Or you can have a £10-million-a-year business and do very well for yourself.

Lifestyle startups turn a profit, rather than just burning money for long periods of time. Burning money puts you in the red, whereas making money puts you in the black. Lifestyle startups bleed black, not red.

Lifestyle startups are businesses that are sometimes local, serving customers in a limited geographic area (for example, you can't get a dental check-up and deep clean over the internet – not yet anyway!). Or they may be more niche (serving customers who have a specific hobby, or who are in a specific business). In other words, their target market is usually smaller.

Here are a few more examples of lifestyle startups or businesses:

▶ Dental surgery
▶ Clothing boutique
▶ Restaurant
▶ Artisan bakery
▶ Architect firm

Notice something interesting? None of these examples are radical, new, or sexy and are generally slow and steady and limited in scale except by replication. In fact, 'startups' as a term is not usually associated with these traditional businesses but rather with tech startups, Silicon Valley, apps, websites and hi-tech gadgets.

However, any small business can be seen through a startup lens, and many digital and technology startups are actually lifestyle businesses. Here are a few examples:

▶ Mobile app development agency
▶ Social media marketing agency
▶ Search engine marketing consultancy
▶ YouTube comedy channel
▶ Online news media publication
▶ Niche software and app startups
▶ Online t-shirt business
▶ Online affiliate marketing

These non-geographically constrained lifestyle businesses are the type serving a small micro-niche, with special interest products, often digital (but as logistics and 'drop-shipping' improves more and more as a model, even physical products are part of this). In other words, if the market is small and the magnitude of the product, i.e. the profit it generates, is limited, the startup won't be large enough to be a hyper-growth business and therefore will not generate much investor interest. There isn't a big enough 'pie' for investors to take a piece of.

Such startups can also include very scalable businesses like Fare Exchange, one of Ash's startups, where the decision is not to raise any external funding but to bootstrap instead.

One example of this latter type is Basecamp, which we mentioned in Chapter 9: Location and Luck. Basecamp used the benefits of *not* being in a startup hub, and used remote staff to its advantage.

Basecamp's founders Jason Fried and David Heinemeier Hansson are great examples of founders who really believe in the benefits of not trying to grow at all costs, of not burning through money, and of not taking on investors. In fact, they have turned down over 100 offers of investment in their project management software over its 18-year history. They have a deliberately relaxed company culture that values a strong work–life balance, with only a 40-hour work week, even for the founders.

This is in stark contrast to the typical VC-funded Silicon Valley approach, which is all about going as hard as possible. In fact, China and its startup hubs, which many experts believe is set to overtake Silicon Valley very soon, became famous for the 9-9-6, that is, working 9am to 9pm, 6 days a week. Even worse, that has now started to be considered lazy in China, and many are doing 12-hour days, 7 days a week. Silicon Valley is looking over and thinking that they need to up the ante on their hustle culture even more to compete.

Hyper-growth startups

Hyper-growth startups are businesses which usually have more of a focus on technology, whether that be in the product itself or in the distribution. For example, Microsoft became so successful and its founder Bill Gates so rich because software is so inherently scalable. Once it's built, it can be distributed at incredibly low cost.

The same can be said for intellectual property such as a film, a book, or photography.

Unlike physical products, for which there is a significant cost in producing each one, for intellectual property and digital products there are a lot of resources spent on the initial creation, but once up and running these digital products can be mass produced at very little cost. So, for example, Adobe may have spent millions making the software Photoshop, but once it was made, they incurred hardly any cost when selling it. It's just a digital download.

When we talk about software we also include smart-phone apps. App startup companies have been getting a lot of attention for some time now, and for good reason. Hyper-growth startups have their roots in software-based or algorithmic innovation. They are built with the expertise of software engineers, designers, and product managers. But to begin with, it's just the founders themselves, though preferably at least one of the founders will have the technical know-how to build and iterate (improve progressively each version of) a digital product based on the needs of users and therefore have the Insight to figure out how to do this.

So, in order to increase your chances of success, in your founding team you need somebody who has the technical Education and Expertise, and somebody who has the Intelligence and Insight to find a gap in the market (in other words, an unfulfilled need) and to be able to commercialise and do the marketing and sales required to get some traction.

Here are a few examples of hyper-growth startups:

- ▶ Just Eat
- ▶ WhatsApp
- ▶ Uber
- ▶ Airbnb
- ▶ Google
- ▶ Apple
- ▶ Salesforce
- ▶ Facebook
- ▶ Instagram
- ▶ YouTube
- ▶ Netflix
- ▶ Amazon

These companies grew fast, and apart from the fact that they did exceptionally well to get a lot of traction and grow virally month on month, what was *also* required were the massive amounts of funding and investment they received. This was almost always, at least initially, from rich family members and friends of the founders, or from the founders themselves having the money to put into it.

For example, Jeff Bezos raised a million dollars as seed investment in Amazon in 1995 and 1996 from angel investors, plus his parents had also invested a significant portion of their life savings into his company. (Needless to say, they all did incredibly well out of this investment.)

So Status, Money, and Location and Luck (right place, right time) are also very valuable here – although you don't necessarily need all of these unfair advantages to succeed. Status can also be built with Intelligence and Insight, and Education and Expertise.

Which type to choose?

So now that you know about the difference between lifestyle and hyper-growth startups, hopefully you can see which one is right for you.

The most important thing for a hyper-growth startup is for its product to *actually* be what customers or users want. This is referred to as 'product-market fit'. That means the market wants the product, they're a good fit. When a startup has product-market fit, its demand will keep increasing and it will grow.

However, the second most important thing for hyper-growth startups to sustain that 'hockey-stick' growth curve is to get funding. They often bleed red, for a long time – in some ways you can look at it as an exercise in burning money. The reason hyper-growth startups lose so much money is because they prioritise satisfying that demand and grabbing as much market share as possible, *as quickly as possible*. This means even if they're making a loss.

Reid Hoffman and Chris Yeh call this 'Blitzscaling' in their book of the same title: 'Blitzscaling means prioritising speed over efficiency, in an environment of uncertainty … in order to reach scale quickly,' they explain.

The reason for this seemingly crazy strategy is that in some industries, investors and founders will determine that there is essentially only going to be one startup that will emerge as the big winner. For example, Google won the search engine game, Facebook won the social media game, Uber (in much of the world) won the on-demand taxi game, Airbnb won the rental accommodation game, Netflix won the subscription streaming video game, and so on and so on.

Basically, these companies might have one, or at a stretch, two competitors who are still in the game – but they're usually way ahead of them anyway.

And because of this dynamic, investors plough millions of dollars of funding into these hyper-growth startups in the hope that they'll hit the home run and become the unicorns in their industries.

This is the premier league of startups. Getting funded by a venture capitalist means you're in the big league, but *getting funded doesn't mean that you've succeeded*. In fact, you're still much more likely to be a zero than a hero.

But to even be in with a chance, you really have to be able to get to that stage, through bootstrapping yourself (having money), through building your status and credibility (through expertise), and building your connections (your status). You're also likely to need to move to a tech startup hub (location), and, most importantly of all, you need to reach the stage of having some *traction* – which comes from creating a product that people actually want.

Money and status (credibility and connections) are the keys to getting funding for hyper-growth startups in the very early stages. With these unfair advantages, you'll have the capital and the connections, and the ability to convince people of your credibility. And credibility comes from having an Insight into a problem, and having some expertise on how to solve that problem.

Hyper-growth startups are better if you're very strong on unfair advantages.

Lifestyle startups are better if your unfair advantages are not so developed.

We'll end with a tweet from a VC, Villi Iltchev:

'If you think you can build a $100M biz, raise VC and go for it. Otherwise, build a $10M biz with $3M in cash flow and live happily ever after.'

Founder mental health

One important note before we move on is something that's often overlooked, and that's taking care of your mental health when getting into entrepreneurship, and even more so if you're aiming to launch a hyper-growth startup.

Every investor that you have on board is added pressure on you. They don't invest in you out of the goodness of their hearts – they want to make a ridiculous amount of money out of your startup. They need their returns on investment. That's their job. So they will sometimes feel like a boss that's breathing down your neck.

The sheer amount of resilience you need to take all the rejections, and take on all the difficulties and obstacles is great.

However, it is very fulfilling and very doable. Entrepreneurs, in general, are not cut from a different cloth. Yes, potentially the outlier success stories like the Collison brothers, Elon Musk, Sara Blakely and Melanie Perkins (co-founder of Canva, see Chapter 17) might be extra lucky, and extra gifted. But we don't need to be on the cover of magazines and to have founded unicorns to consider ourselves a success.

Make sure you get some help and speak to somebody if the pressure gets too much. Make sure you look after the essentials: sleep, nutrition, exercise, relationships, and meditation or spirituality. These are the things that will help keep you sane on this crazy journey. And finally, make sure you are operating within the right environment. This is where the virtual and metaphorical location plays a big role. By locating yourself in the midst of positive, determined and encouraging peers and mentors, you are far far more likely to stay sane and succeed.

14

The idea

'Uber is such a clever idea! At the tap of a button, a car comes to pick me up and take me where I want to go. If only I'd thought of that!'

You hear this sort of thing all the time. People believe that a startup succeeds based on it having a ground-breaking, genius new idea, like Uber. In fact, *execution* is the real differentiator between an idea that remains an idea, and an idea that goes on to become a successful startup.

First of all, ideas are overrated. Yes they're important, but there are countless people all over the world having the same genius ideas at the same time, and the overall conversion rate from idea to successful startup is close to zero.

Secondly, it's a myth that they need to be completely unique and new to be successful.

Most startups are either a twist on an idea that already exists, or the implementation of the same idea but in a new market or industry.

And as we covered under Location and Luck, a lot of it also has to do with timing.

Google wasn't the first search engine. In fact, there were so many search engines at the time (Lycos, Alta Vista, AskJeeves,

Yahoo) that nobody was interested in funding another one. The idea of having a search engine was nothing new, nothing special, and nothing unique. The special thing about it, however, was the Insight that Larry Page and Sergey Brin had – that you can create more relevant and more trustworthy results by looking at how many other sites are linking to that website. The algorithm they created to do that came from their Intelligence, Education and Expertise.

Likewise, Facebook wasn't the first social network. There was already Sixdegrees, Hi5, Orkut, Bebo, Myspace, Friendster, Friends Reunited, plus many many more.

Facebook was in the right place, at the right time. It was set up in Harvard where Mark Zuckerberg was a student, arguably the most prestigious university in the world, and started off being *exclusive* to Harvard students. This gave users of 'The Facebook' (as it was called back then) massive status and exclusivity. Then it rolled out to other elite Ivy League universities first, before being open to every university and eventually to everyone. That way, Zuckerberg was able to build up the network effects of new users connecting with existing users and making it worthwhile for new users to join because 'all my friends are on there'.

This definitely helped Facebook gain the initial traction it needed to grow. The timing was also perfect, as the previous social networks had educated users about how such sites worked. In addition, it was coming in just as broadband was just taking off, and smartphones were entering the scene, allowing people to take selfies and photos and put them on their profiles.

Facebook was the perfect storm of the right unfair advantages. It also had the right founder personality (Mark Zuckerberg's extremely competitive, intelligent and obsessive nature) and the right mentors (Mark had so many great mentors, from

Sean Parker – founder of Napster – to Peter Thiel – Paypal co-founder).

What's more, the strategy that Zuckerberg and his team followed at Facebook, i.e. to roll it out in a controlled way starting from Harvard, then from university to university, then to the public, avoided the main reason that Friendster failed. Friendster had uncontrolled growth, which caused it to be unable to cope with the demand. The company's technological infrastructure couldn't handle all the traffic to its servers, resulting in a bad experience for users when the site wouldn't work properly. Facebook was able to build out its infrastructure more gradually.

Dropbox wasn't the first cloud storage. In the dotcom bubble era, there was a cloud storage startup that failed because it was started a decade too early, when internet connections were still too slow.

Spotify wasn't the first on-demand music platform – you had iTunes before it, and you had Napster even before iTunes. So the idea of music with an unlimited selection and near instantaneous playing of whatever you wanted had been around as an idea since at least 1999, and the only difference with Spotify were the subscription and advertising business models attached to it.

Amazon wasn't the first eCommerce startup (not even the first one to sell books online), and China's Alibaba wasn't the first business-to-business wholesale eCommerce startup.

If you simply start paying attention to successful businesses, from unicorns to successful traditional companies, you'll notice that it's not usually the case that the idea in-and-of-itself is ground-breaking. It's more the execution of it, including leveraging a lot of unfair advantages to succeed.

Consider that it may actually be *worse* for you to be the first in any industry. All these businesses learned from the failures of first-movers in their respective fields. As Amory Lovins, physicist, scientist and writer puts it: 'The pioneers take the arrows, the settlers take the land.'

As Lovins's quote implies, although a completely innovative idea can move entire industries forward in leaps and bounds, the risk to the early movers is much higher. They often have to be the ones to educate the market about the product (or service – for simplicity, in this book we will refer to both as product), which can be very expensive. Look at Palm Pilots, which were basically the first smartphones back in the late 1990s. They never really took off in a big way. Meerkat was the first big mobile livestreaming platform, but then was killed by Twitter buying Periscope (a competitor), and other platforms introducing live streaming such as when Facebook launched Facebook Live. Snapchat itself simply had its innovative ideas (particularly stories) stolen by Facebook and implemented into all their products (Instagram, Facebook, Facebook Messenger, and WhatsApp) when Evan Spiegel refused to sell his business to Facebook. So especially now, in the internet age when a lot of the barriers to launching a startup have come down, going first can be a disadvantage. The giants can simply rip off your idea and implement it as a feature.

Going back to Google, the first amazing thing they achieved was to get it to work so well (through the citation method we mentioned earlier – by looking at the links going to a website). The second amazing thing was their innovative advertising model. This is how they were able to monetise (make money from) their ultra-popular search engine. The way the advertising model works is that they allow businesses to appear at the top of search results in the form of ads, and the business pays every time a user clicks on it. Google actually 'stole' this idea from Bill Gross's startup Overture, which simply ranked the search results based on how much each business paid. The twist Google added was that they introduced a quality and relevance score which helped rank the ads, just as they ranked the normal search results. So Google gained their advantage by taking an idea and running with it, making it better.

So, to reiterate, your idea doesn't necessarily have to be totally unique or ground-breaking, but of course, it is still very important.

How, though, do you come up with a good idea?

You get a great idea by having both a key insight into a problem, and then coming up with a great solution to that problem. This solution is your product. The process by which you get there is a combination of critical and creative thinking, and this often comes from your long-term problem-solving either in a theoretical context (Education advantage) or a practical one (Expertise advantage).

Intersectionality, as we discussed in the section on creative intelligence in Chapter 8, is where ideas come from. Great ideas come when you put a twist on existing things, consider a problem from another point of view, or take a solution from one industry and apply it to another, or from one geographic region to another.

Once you have attuned yourself to thinking in an intersectional way, and learned to look for pain points and solutions, you'll find that ideas come easily. You might even be inundated with them. Our friend Rune Sovndahl, co-founder of London-based £30-million-a-year startup Fantastic Services, often complains that he can't make a simple trip to the supermarket without having at least four to five new business ideas while he's there.

This comes about because he has trained his mind to be highly attuned to seeking out inconveniences, issues, time-wasting processes, underwhelming products and gaps in markets. By noticing them, his mind subconsciously tries to come up with solutions to end the inconvenience, or a product that will respond to an unmet need.

If we were to break the ideas process down using the MILES Framework, we'd probably see some innate creative intelligence at work there, which all of us human beings have to varying degrees, but that might not amount to much unless this raw talent is developed into a powerful skillset through repetition and by being a practitioner, i.e. taking action around your ideas and expanding your expertise over time. Ash had so many business ideas that worked and so many that failed, and so did Rune.

What is Rune's unfair advantage? Like Ash, his background starts with him buying and selling stuff while he was a kid at school. As a 43-year-old entrepreneur and CEO who has launched multiple businesses before, he's had a lot of experience launching a string of 'side hustle' startups, including a fashion content business, a telecoms firm offering cheap phone calls, and dedicated music and dance teacher websites – all while working in managerial roles for the likes of corporates like BT and lastminute.com. So you can see how his experience and expertise built up over the years, plus he gets insights by working in companies, in addition to the all-important mindset factor of seeking to solve everyday problems.

Again, what you have to ask yourself is: What is the problem you are going to solve?

Start with who, not what

One approach which can be very valuable when trying to brainstorm a startup idea is to picture a person for whom you would like to solve a problem. Sometimes it's a problem that they don't know they have because they're so used to having to deal with it, or avoid having to deal with it, that they just see it as an unchangeable fact of life.

As an example, before the invention of the printing press by Johannes Gutenberg around 600 years ago, books were incredibly expensive because each copy needed to be painstakingly written out by hand. Most people at the time would have just considered this a fact of life – that books and learning were only for the wealthy elite because of how expensive they were.

The same can be said of many if not most inventions and innovations. Most people didn't know they 'needed' a computer, or that they 'needed' the internet, let alone needing to have it on a supercomputer in their pocket. Most people didn't realise they needed an online social network, or an on-demand taxi service, or that they needed to be able to buy groceries on their phones.

So it takes a lot of Intelligence and Insight, particularly creative intelligence, to be able to find the unmet needs out there in the world that you can come and meet with your product or service.

And, of course, the great news is that Intelligence and Insight can be cultivated. You start with whatever amount of innate 'talent' you're born with, but hard work can beat talent when talent doesn't work hard. So work on this skillset by consistently thinking about what needs are unmet.

How do you unearth these unmet needs?

By looking for pain or inconvenience.

As you go through life, keep your attention highly attuned to whenever somebody mentions something they find annoying, a problem they can't solve or a situation they're struggling with. Also, don't forget to stay attuned to whatever pain or inconvenience you're experiencing yourself, and how you can solve that!

Scratching your own itch

'Scratching your own itch' is a fantastic way to have a head-start in insight. It just means that you're solving a problem that you yourself have. You, the founder, are the target market for the product you want to build. (The itch is the need, and scratching the itch is what solves the need – hopefully your product.). This is what Tristan Walker did with his startup Walker & Co. As we saw in Chapter 8, his Unfair Advantage came from the fact that he was the target customer of his own startup. As an African American man with thick, curly beard hair, his unique insight was that multi-bladed razors were causing more ingrown hairs, razor burn and irritation for people like him. This allowed him to launch his startup Walker & Co., which uniquely and specifically catered for this target market.

Before settling on this idea, Tristan considered a lot of huge problems like worldwide obesity, trucking and freight, and even banking. However, he ended up settling on something that may be smaller in scope, but an idea where he had a clear unfair advantage – *Insight*.

By identifying a target customer, and digging to find an unmet need, you can uncover some great startup ideas. By carrying out informal, on-the-ground, qualitative research, i.e. by speaking to prospective customers directly, you can really get deep into understanding the problem, the emotions around the problem, and see if it's something painful enough or inconvenient enough for you to bother trying to solve it.

The biggest mistake is having a 'solution', a product, then looking for a problem for it to solve. This is more common than you think, as some people are good at creating a product (whether that be a website, an application, or even an invention) but less good at thinking about who's going to actually part with their cash to buy that product.

Meeting and connecting with people face to face is the most powerful way of unearthing an unmet need, and if that's impossible, then speaking to them over the phone can also be good. Essentially, you have to get out from behind your laptop, and into the real world to interact with people. You can also unearth needs in certain industries by working in those industries. This gives you valuable insight and domain expertise. However you get the insight, you need to hold on to it and make it your unfair advantage.

Then, once you have identified the need, use your education and/or expertise to meet that need by coming up with a product or service. Or partner up with someone who has this education and expertise as their unfair advantage if you don't have it yourself. They can be the technical co-founder to your startup.

But there's something else you need to consider when coming up with a startup idea.

Your unfair advantage is you

Product-market fit is a famous concept in startups. Having product-market fit means that your product satisfies a strong market demand – i.e. there are enough people out there who strongly want what you have to offer.

However, an equally important idea is that of 'founder-product-market fit'. Why is this the case? Because early-stage startups' unfair advantages come directly from the founders themselves. As Naval Ravikant, founder and CEO of AngelList states: 'Above "product-market fit" is "founder-product-market fit".'

If you don't have some kind of unfair advantage in the industry in which you intend to do business, then that particular startup idea and target market might not be the right fit for you. Startup success isn't just about choosing the right idea, it's about choosing the right idea *for you*. However, this doesn't necessarily mean you have to have worked in that industry. A fresh perspective can be very powerful as well, as long as you get that industry perspective in some other way, whether through a co-founder or early employee that you hire.

Take Jan Koum, the co-founder of WhatsApp. Koum knew little about marketing and flash, but *lots* about network reliability and having a clear focus. That was Koum's insight: having the most reliable, cross-platform messaging app, which was easy to use and easy to spread virally (it uses your phone's contact list). It was initially just a status update app, but then evolved into a messaging app when push notifications became a feature of iPhones (another example of the power of iteration and going where the market takes you). Even when WhatsApp started to blow up, Koum refused to do press events about the product, claiming it would be a distraction. Instead of trying to learn tactics outside his realm of expertise, Koum found other team members with their own unfair advantages, ones that complemented his. Brian Acton joined as a co-founder when he was able to raise $250,000, because fundraising was something that Brian was stronger in than Jan. Together, this early team improved the company in ways Koum could never have pulled off alone. WhatsApp eventually sold to Facebook for $19 billion.

Another example comes from one of our startup mentees, Louise Broni-Mensah, and her nightlife event discovery and ticketing startup Shoobs. Her vision is to build the largest and most important urban events community in the world, having been the first ever black woman founder to be accepted onto Y Combinator's prestigious incubator in 2014.

As a solo founder, with the odds stacked against her, Louise has been incredibly successful (having increased her users tenfold since launching Shoobs). She had the unfair advantage of being born and bred in a very ethnically diverse part of London within the urban nightlife culture, which gave her incredible insight. She's also lucky enough to have had a passion for and expertise in this field *in combination* with a successful investment banking career.

The intersection of these two domains and areas of expertise helped her gain the unfair advantage of insight and led to the dominance she has gained in this field. She recently secured $200,000 of funding from Morgan Stanley (which is in addition to the follow-on investment she got from Y Combinator) and is based in their startup accelerator in New York.

Both Koum and Mensah chose startups which were not just good ideas, but good ideas that fit their personal unfair advantages.

A mismatch in this type of fit can lead to what entrepreneur (and professor of entrepreneurship) Steve Blank experienced as his biggest failure. It was at a gaming startup called Rocket Science Games. They lost $35 million, and he attributes much of it to the fact that none of the founders were gamers, or had even worked at a gaming company. They ended up making beautiful games that weren't much fun to play.

When Ash left Just Eat, he took a break to spend a lot of time with his four-year-old daughter. During that time, he ran out of ideas for activities to do with her. He had a brainwave, why not do a kids activities subscription box startup? Parents would subscribe and every month they'd get a box full of creative and fun activities for the kids to do! Problem was, Ash had no experience at all with subscription box startups, nor kids-focused startups. At the time, he had nobody in his network who could help him and after six months trying to launch this startup, he decided not to continue pursuing it. It wasn't a good match – he had no strong unfair advantages in this space, apart from the initial insight. However, there are others who have since succeeded with this startup idea, and they were ex-VC and ex-startup founder mums. They had a stronger unfair advantages and a better founder-product-market fit than Ash.

Hopefully these stories have given you some understanding about which kind of idea may be a good fit for you, and which wouldn't. It's very important to bear in mind which ideas you have unfair advantages in.

15

The people

Finding co-founders

It is exponentially more difficult to succeed in your startup as a solo founder. In fact, we'd strongly discourage you from attempting a startup all by yourself. Most human endeavours, business included, are achieved in teams.

The emotional toll of being a solo founder can be enough to drive you crazy and call it quits. It can be very stressful. This is especially true for hyper-growth startups.

Anthony Casalena, sole founder of Squarespace, ran his startup completely on his own for a full three years. Very few are able to achieve something like this with a hyper-growth startup. However, the stress and strain did get to him. He speaks openly about the fact that his startup was completely all-consuming, to the point where he wouldn't even get on a plane because he didn't want to be disconnected from checking whether the server was still functioning. He even started suffering from full-blown panic attacks that came out of the blue.

For a lifestyle startup, being a solo founder is definitely more doable simply due to the slower growth rate. It's more manageable. However, you don't get off completely scot-free. You're probably going to have moments where you are wracked with crises of confidence, stressed by risk of losing big clients, and struggling with the simple uncertainty and risk of entrepreneurship. Hasan was a solo founder, but if you remember from his story, he wasn't able to do it until he got himself an 'accountability partner', another entrepreneur on the journey. Then they could bounce ideas off each other, and simply keep each other's spirits up. Entrepreneurship can be a lonely road. Mentors also help massively – they helped Hasan on his journey, and Ash on his.

If you do decide to go solo, then joining a co-working space can help, as you can meet other startup founders there, and have people around you rather than working from your home or from cafes on your own.

Ultimately, you will be much better off pooling your strengths and unfair advantages with business partners. This is because it is rare to be good at both developing a product, and selling and communicating that product. Usually you'll be better at one than the other.

In a startup founding team, what you need is a creator, a communicator, and (often) a technician.

These three roles can be all rolled up into one person, or two people, or even split up into more than three. However, usually, two or three co-founders are best.

The creator is the visionary who wants to see their product being loved and used by users and customers, and who is focused on 'making a dent in the universe' as Steve Jobs called it.

The communicator is the commercial co-founder who can sell and market, communicate with customers and prospective customers, and feed this back to the team. The communicator is also the one who 'sells' the investment opportunity to investors, and is therefore the chief fundraiser.

And finally the technician is the one who builds the technical side and makes sure it works, whether that be software, an app, a website, or a life-saving drug, or the formulation for a lipstick or foundation. So it could be an engineer, a chemist, a biologist, or a technician of any kind.

Often it's a team of two, one commercial and one technical, with one of the two also taking on the visionary role as well.

A trusted person, one that you get along with, can come in and fill those missing unfair advantages. As mentioned, that's where the MILES Framework can come in handy, to allow you to figure out how you'll get the money, the insights, the expertise and the status to help you build your startup.

So, if you don't already have a co-founder, now is the time to find one.

You can always outsource the technical parts of your business, but if the technical side is the core of your business, such as in a technology startup that is relying on software, then outsourcing it is not a great idea. This is because you won't be able to easily change, iterate, tweak and evolve your product if you've outsourced it. It'll cost you money every time.

Finding and selecting the right co-founders to turn your idea into a successful startup is one of the most powerful applications of the MILES Framework. What you need to be asking yourself is: Where am I weakest? Which of the Unfair Advantages do I have the least leverage in?

So if you want to do a hyper-growth startup, and you're not very well connected with investors, and not very good at pitching either, maybe you can do as Jan Koum did when he brought in Brian Acton, who was the guy who was actually able to raise the funding. Jan was instead the technical and visionary founder, with Brian as the communicator.

The same happened for Mark Zuckerberg and Facebook. Eduardo Saverin was his co-founder, largely because he was a better networker, communicator and was more commercial, coming from a successful entrepreneurial family. Later on, Sheryl Sandberg filled this more commercial role as Mark continued to be the visionary and creator, as well as the technical founder.

At Apple, Steve Jobs was the visionary and Steve Wozniak was the technical co-founder.

This is a pattern you'll see in many successful startups.

We often get asked how to find a co-founder. Even more often, we get asked how to find a technical co-founder.

That's where you need to network, and be in the right place at the right time. So you need a bit of Location and Luck to help you out, whether it's a physical location (a startup hub, or a technical university) or an online location (virtual communities where you hook up with people).

You can meet potential co-founders in relevant meetups, events, seminars, conventions and exhibitions. Just think about where the person you want to meet might be hanging out.

At the same time, be careful of just partnering with a stranger. Going into business with somebody is in some ways like marriage, and in the case of a hyper-growth startup, you'll probably see them more than your spouse! It's all about trust, and that takes time to build. Do your due diligence on people, and ideally pick someone you could already trust.

Conflict between startup founders is probably the leading cause of startup death. Be very careful who you go into business with. It helps to have worked on projects with them before, so you can get a sense of how well you work together.

How to grow your network

One of the keys to finding a co-founder, or a mentor, advisor, or investor, is networking, which really just means meeting and building relationships with people.

There are two ingredients needed to develop your network:

1. An authentic desire to add value to people you meet
2. A drive to increase your Status so that people perceive more value from you

Let's define 'value'. In a social and networking context, value is *not* achieved solely by what you can do for someone. For example, if you are a masseuse, you don't have to offer to do free massages. If you're a consultant, you don't need to give a deep-dive into someone's business with a strategy session. It can be as simple as introducing two for whom there is potential mutual benefit from getting to know one another. Or it could be as simple and easy as being warm, courteous and respectful, and a good listener.

Avoid falling into the trap of being too picky about whom you add value to, and 'saving' your value for only those you think are relevant. For example, if you're at a startup event, and you meet somebody you don't think will benefit you in some way, be careful about brushing them off in order to meet somebody you can get value from. This can put you in completely the wrong mindset and you will unconsciously come across as selfish and unkind.

That's the thing about social interactions – spreading positive emotions, even if it's simply a warm smile, costs you nothing, and pays you dividends.

You might be rolling your eyes right now, because while we can make it sound easy, to the introverts among you especially, networking is something you dread. As an introvert, Hasan has pushed himself to meet more people and expand his network, and many introvert entrepreneurs have taught themselves to break out of their shells to build more relationships.

You might be thinking 'Won't giving "value" to as many people as possible be too time-consuming?'

As you develop further in your entrepreneurial journey, you need to become more judicious with your time, which will become increasingly scarce. But for the meantime, it's the one thing that you probably have more of than the person you're talking to. Giving up time in order to reap the benefits of experience and wisdom seems like a small sacrifice. Yet some people think they don't even have time to say hi – and that's why we say value can simply mean being pleasant, interested and warm.

Networking shouldn't be a salesy handing out of business cards. Make it a genuine desire to learn about people and listen. If you listen closely, you may be able to get great insights that help uncover business needs and reveal other perspectives.

Realise that most people you'll meet are operating at the 'what's in it for me' level, but that you yourself need to notice when you're thinking in those terms, and try to broaden your value-adding outlook to go beyond that.

That being said, if you have specific business or career goals, be careful of being too indiscriminate with your networking, as you can spend hours at networking events simply being pitched at and sold to by people who are trying to recruit you for their benefit in some way.

It's not all about the breadth of your network, it's also about the depth. Deeper relationships mean stronger relationships and a stronger network. Having 5,000 LinkedIn contacts isn't worth much if none of them reply to your message. That's why it's always helpful, at least at first, to be introduced by someone – someone who can endorse you, who can vouch for your talent or even just knows your name. The person to whom you want to talk is much more likely to listen if they've met you that way. Cold contact (without a warm introduction) is the least powerful way of growing your network, but can still work if what you are offering is interesting enough to your listener.

The strength of your network increases the more you add value to it.

You can add more value to your network by proactively reaching out to people periodically, and not just when you want something from them.

You can literally set up a daily habit of reaching out to one relevant person from your network simply to add value, even if in a small way such as by asking how they are, or forwarding them an article, or commenting on a status they've put on a social media network. For professional networks, LinkedIn of course is king, and is a great way to add value, find people's relevance to you, and stay up to date with what they're doing. It's also a great way to get introductions – a very powerful way of increasing your network.

How to get mentors – by Hasan

People often ask me how I attract successful multimillionaire entrepreneurs as mentors.

They're usually expecting some kind of magic-bullet response.

The reality is that there is no magical way to get a mentor – it's simply the ability to build a relationship with someone of higher status than you. Good mentors are incredibly busy, and they're constantly being contacted by people who want to simply take, take, take from them. And they're usually so deep in the execution and building and running of their own companies that they can't meet or help every person asking them for advice.

In its extreme form (and unfortunately very common form) this approach is simply leeching.

I get a lot of messages and emails from people asking if they can buy me lunch or a coffee, and Ash gets even more. We couldn't have that many lunches or coffees even if we wanted to.

The successful people are those who seek to add value.

I met Ash at a business dinner, and even though I knew that he had recently been part of a large IPO and was incredibly successful as an entrepreneur and growth hacker, I asked him how I could help *him*.

I am lucky enough to have had this instilled in me by my parents – to always seek ways of helping before asking for help.

And in fact, what probably did me a favour was that I wasn't seeking any help at that time.

Here are some tips on finding a mentor:

1. **Identify who could be a good mentor for you.**
   Remember, you don't need to aim too high, somebody simply a couple years ahead of you on their journey might be enough.

2. **Get their attention – break through the noise.** These people receive huge numbers of messages asking for help and advice, and offers to meet for lunch or coffee so that their brains can be picked. Naturally they put most of these long emails (they're often really long) straight in the junk folder to protect the most valuable thing for them – their time. Bear that in mind. To break through the noise you need to be straight to the point and you need to do Step 3...

3. **Seek to add value.** Just because potential mentors are successful or higher status, this doesn't mean you can't

add value to them. Have faith that you have some way of helping them. Study what they're doing. Are they involved in any philanthropy or social impact causes? How can you help? That's a great way to get their attention.

4. Act *normal*. This applies wherever there's an imbalance of status. For example, when you meet somebody that you're interested in romantically, and you feel as if they're probably 'out of your league', you have to not let that make you behave strangely. If you are too deferential, too reverent, and basically tripping over yourself to do stuff for them because you perceive them to be on another level, then they are unlikely to feel attracted to you. And conversely, sometimes acting 'not normal' means you go the other way, and behave like a schoolboy pulling the pigtails of the girl he fancies, and going too far in overcompensating. Again, that is not good.

There has to be a sort of 'normalness' to your interactions with a potential mentor. Acting naturally and not letting their higher status get to you is the way forward.

So even if you feel that you need a mentor quite badly, play it a bit cool. Not so cool that you seem aloof, arrogant and immune to their expertise, but not desperate either. Desperation doesn't work. The hungry don't get fed. That's why celebrities get free meals, free designer dresses, and people paying to be around them.

Be pleasant to be around.

5. **Apply** what your mentor advises you to do **as quickly as possible**, then immediately feed back to them the outcome of the action.

This feedback loop will generate and strengthen the mentor-mentee relationship in the fastest possible way, because entrepreneurial mentors love coachable people who take action. And they feel more and more responsibility when they're the ones directing your action and you're coming back to them to report what happened. It's like an interesting and fun game for them, and they want to know that they're helping you in a tangible way.

Be coachable.

And if you really need expert help in the meantime, seriously consider paying for it while you're searching for your ideal mentor. That's the ultimate shortcut. If you're blessed with money to invest, then spending it on expert guidance can save you years and years of trial and error. Strong experts and people with genuine know-how are usually practitioners, and their time is incredibly valuable. I've invested thousands of pounds in advice, education and guidance over my entrepreneurial career, and it has definitely paid off. If you haven't got the cash immediately, then look online, follow people you admire, read books, join forums. Do your homework, and don't hesitate to invest in progressing both your mind and your business to the next level.

16

The business

Whether you want to build a Lifestyle startup or a Hyper-Growth startup, you need to start small – take small risks by running small tests to see if your idea has legs. That means not risking significant sums of money on it straight away.

The common mistake is to have an idea (hopefully based on an actual need in the market) and then immediately go out to try to get funding for it. In some traditional businesses, such as a restaurant or physical location store, it may need to be that way – but even for them we'd highly recommend starting with less capital-intensive pop-up shops and street food markets to give yourself the opportunity to test whether people actually like what you're offering, before taking the plunge to plough huge amounts of money into the idea.

For businesses that don't need a physical location, it is particularly unwise to start fundraising for an idea immediately – if only because it's now so easy to start your business and test your idea first. With the world of digital, the barriers to starting a business have been reduced. For example, if you wanted to start a business selling your own brand of makeup, you could simply start with an Instagram page and a Shopify website. You could even get white label (sometimes called private label) companies to take care of the whole product side of it for you, and another company to handle your payments and delivery, and logistics. That's what Kylie Jenner did (see Chapter 11).

Rather than looking for fundraising from the start, then, the course of action we'd recommend is to 'bootstrap' your startup. Bootstrapping comes from the idea of 'pulling yourself up by your bootstraps'. In other words, you did it by yourself. No outside help in the sense that you had no external investors. It usually implies that you fund your startup a little from your own savings, and then use the cash flow from the money you make from customers to fund further growth.

Lifestyle startups can stay perpetually bootstrapped in most cases (except if they're particularly capital intensive and require large assets such as machinery or property/land), whereas hyper-growth startups usually do need investment. But even most hyper-growth startups should aim to bootstrap, at least at the beginning.

In 2007, Jan Koum had a whopping $400,000 of personal savings when he left Yahoo, and was thinking about his next steps. Some of this money helped fund the early days of WhatsApp. After nine months of Koum growing the company and with a quarter of a million users already (without any external funding), Brian Acton joined the startup and helped raise a 'friends and family' seed round of $250,000 – mostly from ex-colleagues who also worked at Yahoo. This is an example of highly effective bootstrapping, and even if you don't have family and friends who can invest thousands into your project, like Jan you can try to partner with someone who does.

It is in this early bootstrapping phase that creativity and resourcefulness are of most value, as you have to be creative in how you get your startup off the ground without burning all your money.

The idea validation phase

Once you have your idea, it's time to validate it – to check if there are actually people out there who want to buy what you're selling, or users who want to actively use your product. Then, based on user/customer feedback you have to tinker and tweak and rethink your approach to make it just right for them.

You need them to *love* your product, not just *like* it. They need to be your evangelists, they need to spread the good news by word of mouth. If they don't, then you're probably going to fail. Word of mouth is like striking gold, because word of mouth is free and if you have enough of it, you'll have viral growth.

So this is the early phase of your startup. You have to split your time doing only two things almost exclusively: building your product and speaking to your customer. That's it. The next section talks about building your product (your Minimum Viable Product), but before you do that, first try to find out if people will actually be interested.

Speaking to your customer includes selling and marketing to them, whereas building your product includes developing the products and services that you'd like to sell.

Ideally, you could get a letter of intent or even pre-orders, which might be possible if you were to crowdfund an exciting idea. The letter of intent works especially well for enterprise ideas (i.e. if the customers are big companies). This is the closest you can get to real validation before going ahead and building your product.

If it's a web design or app development agency you want to run (a lifestyle business), then you have to simply go and speak to your potential customers, and do anything to get some traction, get a first sale, even if you don't make a profit from it.

You need to learn the process, what customers like and don't like, what different customers want from you.

The only way to learn is to dive in at the deep end.

The same is true if you want to build a hyper-growth startup, such as one that targets people who are having trouble losing weight. You have to speak to the customers, get your products in their hands, and see if it helps to solve their problem. You have to figure out how you need to tweak the product for them to love it and see if your tech-based solution can do the job – for example, by helping them plan and track their meals with an app.

Often your idea simply won't work.

You may have created a solution for a problem that doesn't really exist, or for a problem the customers don't perceive as a problem, or for a small problem that the customer is not motivated to solve.

The mistake most of us make is that we envision that our solution is going to be loved. We fall in love with our own idea. This is very dangerous. Beware of falling in love with your idea before you have any feedback from prospective customers/users.

You have to have a scientific mindset and simply look at the empirical data. Do people want to part with money to buy your product or not? If it is a free app that will monetise by other means (e.g. advertising) and be funded directly by the user, you have to see whether people are using it regularly. If not, you have to figure out why not by speaking to users and analysing the data of their behaviours.

You then need to iterate (tweak and improve) your idea or product based on customer feedback. This iterative process is extremely important. In fact, often startups realise that they need to make a big change, which is known as a pivot.

WhatsApp did this. It was initially an idea based on giving

your current status (for example: I'm at the gym, I'm busy, do not disturb, I'm abroad, etc.). It later pivoted into a messaging app once iPhone released push notifications.

Instagram also pivoted. It was initially called Burbn and was designed to let users check in at particular locations or bus inesses. It pivoted into Instagram when they saw how popular their photo-sharing feature was, especially the innovative filters.

Idea validation is still the early stage of your startup. Even if you've built a product, you probably won't be making any significant money at this point, particularly if you are trying to do a hyper-growth startup.

That's why, as we mentioned, it's important to bear in mind your cash flow and runway time to make sure you don't run out of money. Startup founders often simplify their lifestyles to lower their expenses, or build up a good amount of savings which allows them to pay their bills and living expenses without an income for a few months. And that's why it's good to start off doing it as a 'side hustle', a startup that you begin bootstrapping in your spare time while keeping a full-time job.

This is a good time to remind you that you can even freelance as a way to support yourself. There are so many websites out there nowadays that allow you to make money by selling your skills online on a project-by-project basis, or even being paid by the hour to work for a client remotely. Whether you can code, write articles, do social media management or marketing, consult small businesses and other startups, or do some great design, there are opportunities out there for you.

If it is a lean lifestyle business you're setting up, you can often start making money very quickly, but it will be a very steep learning curve unless you have some kind of expertise in an area that people want help with and are willing to pay for.

This can be a 'solo-preneur' type of business; in other words, a freelancer operation. Many digital nomads are freelancers or one-person businesses who build a virtual team of project-based workers.

Whether you're launching a product or service, you should always follow the next step, building an MVP.

Building an MVP (Minimum Viable Product)

To get your business started, you need to build a minimum viable product. Let's break this down.

Minimum means simplified. It means without bells and whistles, just core features. A core purpose that it needs to achieve – solving the problem, meeting the need that you've uncovered with your idea. As we've said, this of course applies to services as well as products.

If you're just starting out and want to learn by doing, just focus on the core value proposition. With your first client and initial contract, if the client wants to boost their Instagram followers, for instance, resist the urge to try to sell them a website as well if you haven't got the expertise or talent to do that yet. Initially, focus on exactly what they came to you for, and don't be distracted by trying to do more. This will allow you to more easily get the sale, and to learn the process by doing it. After that you can add more to your service offering and create packages.

For product, especially software like websites and apps, this minimal approach avoids you spending years developing something before it sees the light of day.

You have to build something that's crappy, but that works.

Crappy?

Yes. In most industries, especially the ones where you're specifically solving a strong problem, it doesn't matter if the product doesn't look good (unless looking good is the need it is meeting). It doesn't matter if it sometimes crashes and restarts itself as an app. It doesn't matter if it has typos and mistakes. What matters is whether it solves the problem or not.

This way of thinking, which doesn't apply to every single case, is often very helpful – it can put a stop to the perfectionism, fear and procrastination that can hold you back from launching your business.

Hasan really struggled with the scourge of perfectionism when starting out, and it took him an extra nine months before he could launch, simply because of that fear and perfectionism.

However, if you're the type of person who's ever encumbered by the need for perfectionism, and you don't take care to make sure your product actually meets the need it intends to meet, then you should probably not listen to this advice and instead take some pride in your work.

The former is so much more common and that's why LinkedIn co-founder Reid Hoffman says 'If you're not embarrassed by the first version of your product, you've launched too late.' Mind you, he doesn't say 'deeply ashamed'. But with hindsight you should be looking back on your first version as pretty crappy.

At Just Eat, Ash found that it was not uncommon for him to hear criticism from his repeat customers about the website and the way it worked. They'd say 'Ash, your website is rubbish'. Funnily enough, this was a good sign that they were onto something with their idea, because if customers didn't like the interface of the website very much, but were still using it, it showed that it was genuinely meeting an unmet need for them.

So get your webshop launched with only a few products. Get your t-shirt business launched with only a few designs. Get your app launched with only a few simple features, and even if the website or app is not super-slick straight away, understand that because this is all digital, they can easily be tweaked very quickly and improved.

A strategy that many entrepreneurs use is to create marketing and attempt to sell a product that's still in develop ment. They make it appear as if their new product is ready to buy, but in fact they're only testing to see if people are happy to part with their money. Only once the customer attempts to make the purchase does the website or app let them know that this product is not available yet and gives them the option to pre-order it. Obviously we would only recommend this if you do it in an ethical and undeceiving way, but it can be a very interesting approach to validating an idea, and potentially even funding its production as well.

It's very important to iterate and evolve your product, and even pivot if you have to, based on real feedback from your customers or users.

Sara Blakely did this right. She designed Spanx, her product, using real women – who would give her actual feedback – rather than employ the then industry standard of using mannequins. This brilliant approach helped her enjoy astounding success, because just like successful tech startups do nowadays following idea validation, she iterated quickly and got real feedback.

This feedback allowed her to design an ever-expanding line of garments including more innovations such as Arm Tights, meant to help women wear their sleeveless clothes all year round.

That is the right way to develop a product. Just make sure you don't spend months and months building it before it sees the light of day and before you've validated your idea.

Growth scrapping

Ash is known as a 'Growth Hacker'. It means that he is great at making a startup grow fast. Startup founders often ask him: how do I do growth hacking?

Ash's answer? Before growth hacking, you've got to do growth scrapping.

What does this mean?

It means that before you think about doing big scalable marketing campaigns using Google and Facebook ads, you need to creatively find each of your early customers/users manually.

In this early stage, before you've reached the stage of product-market fit (which is when word of mouth helps you grow virally), you need to really 'hustle'. You need to manually, one-by-one, get your first set of customers or clients. Preferably you do this face to face, or at least directly through person-alised messages and outreach using social media and email.

And make sure you don't spam them!

Hustle in a clever way by doing your homework on each person. Realise that you're going to get a lot of rejections and that you'll need to develop a thick skin. This is called marketing, sales and business development.

Mindset is critical at this stage. Being resilient. Having the vision to motivate yourself. Having the determination, perse-verance and grit to just get on with it and unearth an unmet need.

Paul Graham of Y Combinator perfectly describes what you need to do at this stage when he says 'Do things that don't scale'. That means don't try to use technology to make your job easier, but instead do it in a more time-consuming, person-to-person kind of way. For example, rather than trying to spam out an email to hundreds of people, do it manually one-by-one, crafting and personalising each email to match each person. Meet people face to face. Call people on the phone. Go out of your way to get sales and keep customers happy, rather than worrying that you won't be able to scale this later.

Another way you can apply this edict of 'do things that don't scale' is to give amazing customer service to your early users/customers. Don't worry too much that as you grow, you won't be able to keep up this level of customer service, because hopefully by then your product will have improved to the point that fewer people will need that service.

You growth scrap to build some traction, to build some momentum and forward progress in your startup.

How do you do that? You make sure that you measure your growth and focus on it every day. You concentrate on sales, and product development based on customer feedback, to make your customers love your product even more.

But be careful about measuring what's often referred to as vanity metrics. Vanity metrics are numbers that may be growing, but which don't represent the most important thing for you to measure. For example, social media followers, or the number of likes you get. For most startups, high numbers of social media followers in the early days isn't going to amount to much. Instead you need to focus on getting sales or downloads of your app.

Another vanity metric is simply counting the number of new users or customers, and not checking retention. This is relevant for apps, software and subscription products. If you're not retaining your customers, i.e. they are not coming back to you or staying subscribed, it could be a bad sign, so make sure you measure how many customers/users stay the course.

'What about growth hacking?' – by Ash

Growth hacking is something I've become known for and what I'm asked about *all the time*. However, most founders asking me this question are way too early in their startup to think about growth hacking. Growth hacking is *after* there is solid product-market fit, which means your product is so attuned to what customers want that it's starting to spread by word of mouth. Your customers really *love* it.

It usually takes time to get to that stage and that's why we talk about 'growth scrapping' first.

Growth hacking is a term coined by Sean Ellis in 2010 to distinguish it from digital marketing. It refers to a set of both traditional and unconventional marketing and product development experiments that lead to growth. It's something that's become synonymous with fast-growing startups. Growth hackers are focused on only one goal: growth. This is usually tracked by what we call the North Star Metric, a key metric which defines the core value proposition of a company.

Why 'hacking'? The word has several meanings, good and bad. In the context of growth hacking, a 'hack' means a clever kind of shortcut that can get you better results, faster. Often, good 'hackers' have a multi-disciplinary skillset and are good at understanding data.

Wikipedia describes growth hacking as 'a process of rapid experimentation and testing across marketing channels and product development to identify the most effective, efficient ways to grow a startup rapidly'. Which basically means you find one or two great marketing acquisition channels and double-down on them, then continue to develop good organic growth features in your product or service, e.g. a refer-a-friend scheme. At the heart of growth hacking is creativity.

Growth hacking is the intersection between creativity,

marketing and tech. It requires a 'testing, fail, repeat, test, fail repeat, scale' mindset.

There are plenty of stories of well-known startups using growth hacks to grow quickly, such as Airbnb taking advantage of Craigslist, and Hotmail adding the line 'PS: I Love You. Get your free email at Hotmail' at the end of every email sent. At Just Eat, we used Google Maps listings and our restaurant reviews as a very powerful growth hack.

However, many of these growth hacks had their time and won't work in exactly the same way again. There are no growth hack 'silver bullets'. What's important about growth hacking is the mindset – to keep experimenting and tinkering with your tactics.

And remember that what worked in the past will often not make you a success today. That's why the mindset is more important than the tactics and why being a growth hacker means unlearning and relearning all the time.

The true growth hacker has a growth *mindset*. They are not attached to any particular marketing or distribution channel. They are not in love with what worked in the past. They are looking at the world as it is, assessing options, testing often, and then making a move on what works best.

Ultimately the most important thing is to get the fundamentals right, which means having an excellent product or service that makes customers happy.

Once you have that, you have product-market fit. Only then should you think about growth hacking to scale your growth and inject more fuel (usually money) onto the fire.

17

Fundraising

If you've decided you will need external funding for your startup, this chapter is a quick primer on the topic based on our experience, and from speaking to other investors.

Fundraising can be a subject with many intricacies, but your job as founder is not to concern yourself with too many of these. Your job is to focus on making a startup that's investable.

So instead of little details about 'convertible notes' and the ins and outs of a term sheet, in the beginning you simply need to focus on the fundamentals.

With that in mind, in this chapter you'll find lots of lists. We want to pack in as much value for you as possible to get you started strong.

First of all, remember that you're not starting a company to raise money, you're doing it to serve customers, clients or users, and make a profit, and ideally have some kind of positive impact in the world. Always keep that in mind.

It's also important to remember that not every founder or startup needs to raise lots of money. You've probably heard plenty of stories of those who have knocked on hundreds of doors to get that one or two VCs who finally invested. Yet there are thousands of other stories where it simply was a NO time after time.

Many founders we've spoken to over the years have said how gruelling, distracting and time-consuming raising money is, so be ready for the ride!

When asking investors or VCs for funding, it's important to first have traction. That means having fast growth. It's as simple as that. You need to show that month on month, you have been growing very fast, ideally with a 'hockey-stick' growth curve.

The less traction you have in your startup, the more difficult it is, because essentially you're then just asking them to invest in an idea.

A big Unfair Advantage here is a type of Expertise that we haven't discussed directly, but have touched on – raising money for an *idea* is usually the domain of a founder who's done a successful startup already. So serial founders have a huge leg-up here, because they've proven that they can do it before, so investors are likely to believe they can do it again. Without that track record, you'll either have to have a lot of unfair advantages going for you, or you have to rely on getting enough traction first.

Funding a hyper-growth startup often follows this sequence as the startup grows:

1. **Savings** – Often a hyper-growth startup begins with self-funding from the founders' savings. Some founders use credit cards as well, but we wouldn't recommend this as it's very risky.

2. **Bootstrapping** – This is usually the next stage and means that you are using the revenue you generate from customers to fund the startup, as you start making sales.

3. **The Three Fs: Family Friends and Fools** – These are the people who believe in you the most. ('Fools' is a half-joke nod to how often startups fail. But you better not believe

they're fools, hopefully you've fully bought into your startup idea!). Not everyone has rich family and friends who can afford to take the risk on a startup, and that's why this represents the unfair advantage of status. In exchange, these people get equity (shares in your startup).

(By the way, in the UK and in many countries there are tax breaks for investing in startups to encourage more startup investment. Look up the terms SEIS (Seed Enterprise Investment Scheme) and EIS (Enterprise Investment Scheme) for more information.)

4. **Grants and Competitions** – Government grants, Social Impact Funds, crowdfunding, startup competitions, hackathons, etc. – These are all ways you can raise funding, and you can see in the case study of Canva below that their government grant really helped them. This is not usually in exchange for equity (except in the case of crowdfunding where some platforms do it on an equity basis).

5. **Private Angel Investors** – These are essentially rich individuals who invest in startups, usually as a sideline. They're often successful startup founders themselves, like Ash for instance. They are usually the first outside investors, ie, not friends or family. They are often easier to approach and pitch to than VCs, and they have to like your vision and you, the market, and sometimes even the social impact.

6. **Venture Capital** – These are institutions that invest professionally. They are more rigorous than friends and family and invest larger sums of money and at a later stage. They look at your Team, Traction, Growth, and Total Addressable Market (TAM).

7. **Private Equity** – Like VCs, but for more mature companies.

8. **IPO or Acquisition** – Floating on the public stock market or being acquired by a larger company.]/nl[

For early-stage founders in particular, the options should be considered carefully. What is right for you? Maybe you are happy to stop after 1, 2 and 3 – you would have what you need.

If you do decide to go down the angel investor and VC route, here are the top tips we picked up from Silicon Valley, the land of startup funding! The key difference between angels and VCs is that angel investors expect less traction, and therefore their investment is based *even more* on their confidence in the co-founders.

To raise funding, especially VC funding, it is imperative to first know that you really want to raise money and go big. Your intentions really matter at this stage. As we discussed, it can definitely still be very lucrative just being a lifestyle startup if you want to stay local, or artisan, or have a small team, so ensure your mind is completely made up before considering raising funds from VCs. If a VC invests, you'll be accountable to outside shareholders in very significant way.

The first order of business in fundraising is doing your research on which investors you want to target. Don't target every investor without doing any research – different investors invest in different kinds of startups. Make sure you are the type of startup that that angel or VC usually invests in.

Profile your investors to avoid wasting everyone's time. Here is a quick list of things to look at:

1. Industries and businesses – do they usually invest in your kind of startup?

2. Ticket size – how much do they typically invest?

3. Application process – what are the steps you have to follow to apply to them?

4. Decision-making process – what are their criteria for investment?

5. Location – which countries and geographies do they usually invest in?

6. More than just money approach – not all money is equal. Consider your startup needs and reference check investors from previous founders they've worked with. A lot of the supposed 'value add' from investors is oversold.

Once you have identified who you want to go for, try to get a warm introduction. This is when you need to use your networking skills that we discussed in Chapter 15.

Then, it's about pitching.

How to pitch to raise funding

Before we get into the content of your pitch, let's talk about communication. Investors don't have time to figure out what you're trying to say. If your communication is not crystal clear, then you're going to have an incredibly uphill battle. We see this problem a lot from the hundreds of pitches we've listened to ourselves. Please work on making your initial messages, emails and pitch ultra-concise and to the point. Avoid jargon. Speak in simple language. Don't use marketing-speak, as you would with advertising to consumers – that doesn't work on investors and just irritates them. Brevity is key.

To achieve clarity in your communication, you need to be specific. Specificity is ultra-important. Don't say things like 'we're revolutionising social media', say exactly what your startup will do – 'we are getting rid of the newsfeed', for example.

Now, for the content of your pitch, you need to answer the following ten questions:

1. What does your startup do? – The simpler the better.

2. What problem are you solving? – This is where you need to present your key Insight.

3. How big is the market? – This is the Total Addressable Market (TAM). Research it. If it's a completely new product, estimate how big the market is (number of customers x how much you'd charge each customer).

4. What is your traction? – This is how many users, customers or clients you already have. The investor will want to see a very fast growth rate. If you have none, you'd better have at least some evidence that your product is what customers want, even if this is just a handful of customers. You'll also need a 'go-to-market' strategy, meaning a clear and well-thought-through marketing plan if you have no significant traction yet.

5. How will you make money? – This is needs to be clear.

6. Who are the team? – This is mainly to find out about the co-founders themselves. Highlight your individual Status and credibility factors. What you have achieved in your lives so far?

7. Who are your competitors? – Do your research of the competitor landscape. If you say you have no competitors, that makes investors extremely sceptical.

8. What is your Unfair Advantage? – Using the MILES Framework, assess what unfair advantages you have, then decide which one is most relevant. State it in terms of the startup and how your unfair advantage will help make it

a success. For example, 'with our Insight, we are the only ones of all our competitors addressing this specific unmet need'. Or, 'with our strong network in this industry, we are uniquely placed to be able to reach the customers and sell our product to them'.

9. How much money do you want to raise? – You have to be clear on this. If in doubt, raise a bit more than you think you'll need, as this will save you from having to go back and do another round of fundraising

10. What will you spend that money on? – Investors want to hear that you'll spend it on the right things, like sales and marketing and product development.

These ten questions cover virtually everything you'll need for your pitch. You can even have each question as a single slide, and come out with a 9- or 10-slide pitchdeck (the last two can be put on one slide).

Pitching top tips

Learn about the power of storytelling, then use storytelling skills to keep your pitch interesting and coherent.

▶ If you have no traction, then sell your vision and your team, and give some other validation or proof that your product is what customers really want.

▶ Tell them what your growth forecasts are. Savvy investors know that forecasts are inaccurate, but they want to see your thinking behind this more than anything.

▶ If it's VCs you're pitching to, you don't need to spend too much time talking about market size. You need to have done thorough research because they already have plenty of data on this, but VCs will do their own homework. Just make sure the market size is in the billions of dollars if you want VCs to be interested.

▶ Get a strong founding team and tell them why *you* will win in your chosen market. Make sure you highlight your personal unfair advantages.

▶ Try to find investors who really believe in you, rather than those who simply invest based on FOMO (Fear Of Missing Out).

▶ Keep crafting your investor story and customer solution story at key milestones and use two different decks (i.e don't send investors your customer/product demo deck, keep them are separate).

▶ VCs want to bet big, so show them your path to 1, 5, even 100 million dollars in revenue.

▶ Don't forget, ultimately investors care mostly about cash and what return you will give them, that's the bottom line.

▶ A quick way to learn if somebody is interested in your startup is to ask a simple question such as 'can I send you my deck for feedback on slide 7 please?' and then email over a short deck.

▶ Another thing we're seeing more often is the one-pager – a good way to present a concise version of your company as an executive summary.

▶ If you want referrals and introductions, make it easy for someone to refer you by writing them a pre-written email that they can edit and send.

▶ Always try to use a warm intro with VCs – get on their radar, follow their recent investments and read their tweets.

Pitching no-nos

When speaking with investors, keep in mind a few things that put them off and avoid the following:

▶ 'We are building an app, website or MVP' – try to have it already built

▶ 'We don't have competitors' – suggests you just haven't researched enough

▶ 'We are going to be worth £10 million in month 6' – don't go crazy with your valuation

▶ jargon

▶ 'Hurry, we are closing our round now' – creating false scarcity will just irritate people

▶ Complicated pitchdecks with 30 slides – this is too much

▶ 'We haven't tested any of our ideas yet'– test them!

▶ 'Co-founding teams need big salaries'

▶ 'We just need money – not your help' – investors want to feel useful beyond just cash

Now you have founded your startup. You've thought about your goals and your 'why', you've understood the two different kinds of startups, you've come up with an idea, you've found a co-founder, tested your idea, built your MVP, growth scrapped your startup, and also funded it.

Unfair advantages are not static. They don't exist eternally, they develop and change. You should always be asking yourself what your unfair advantages are, both for you and your startup.

A final exciting case study is that of Melanie Perkins, co-founder of Canva, a startup unicorn. Her story perfectly illustrates the un-level playing fields and unfair advantages we've discussed in the book.

Melanie Perkins, Canva – stacking your unfair advantages

This case study is unmissable. We've saved it until the end because it encompasses a lot of the lessons and unfair advantages that you've learned about.

In 2007, Melanie Perkins was a 19-year-old university student in Perth, Australia. She was teaching design programs part-time at university, and she noticed how much students struggled to learn just the basics – it took a whole semester merely to teach them where all the buttons were. Microsoft Publisher and Adobe products were very complex and were old-fashioned desktop-based softwares. That was her Insight.

She had a big vision to take on these behemoth software companies, but as she was only 19, she decided to start by solving a simpler problem that was closer to home.

She noticed that every year her mother, a schoolteacher, was under a lot of stress to manage the high-school yearbook that the students of the class would all collaborate on. These teachers had no design experience and it was all a big headache for them. Melanie knew this could be made easier with online collaborative software. So, she and her boyfriend Cliff Obrecht took out a loan from their family and friends Ð they were privileged enough to be able to raise $50,000 from them, leveraging their Status to get Money. With this money, they interviewed every tech team in Perth to see which one could build the software for them. Most of the tech teams thought these teenagers were completely mad, but finally Melanie and Cliff found one who agreed to take on their project. What they lacked in Status because of their young age, they made up for in persistence and a willingness to learn from their mistakes, and to Educate themselves and build up their entrepreneurial Expertise.

Through a steep learning curve, and by turning Melanie's

mum's living room into the office for the new yearbook design startup Fusion Books (along with large printing press machines), they bootstrapped the project and grew year on year. Once she started employing staff, Melanie gradually took over the house: 'We also took over my mum's garage, driveway and hallway with our 24/7 printing operation. Gee was she gracious.' Speaking of family members helping out, her mum checked the books word for word, her boyfriend's mum did the accounts, and his dad would drive down to pick up the mail from the PO Box.

So you can see all the help and support they got from their family members. In the Status chapter, we learned that sociologists call this social capital.

The Australian government provided R&D tax concessions, and the pair were later able to get an extra $20,000 business bank loan. Melanie says that without these, they'd have run out of money in the early days, and wouldn't have survived.

The next chapter of their story is where it gets really interesting. Serendipity struck, and they met an investor from Silicon Valley, Bill Tai, at an Inventor of the Year awards ceremony (they were runners-up). When they spoke to him, a 5-minute chat opened a window onto a whole new world. Melanie described her grand vision to take on the big design companies of Microsoft and Adobe with her more ambitious hyper-growth startup idea – the online collaborative design software that became Canva – and Bill Tai agreed to meet them if ever they were in Silicon Valley. 'I couldn't believe my luck!' Melanie said.

So she went home and researched this unknown universe of Silicon Valley, venture capitalists and 'startups'. Again, luck played its role, because her brother happened to be studying in San Francisco (which is very close to Silicon Valley), and agreed to let her crash at his for two weeks.

She packed her things and took her big startup idea to the Valley. She was very nervous about the meeting. She dressed up in smart clothes for the meeting with Bill Tai who casually remarked that she needn't have bothered (she described how she was mortified by this). During the meeting, he was actually on his phone texting while she pitched him her big idea, which went way beyond just yearbooks. She was really disappointed Ð she thought he wasn't interested.

In fact, he had been sending out messages to his network to invite her to speak to them and to make introductions.

He finally said that he'd invest, but only if they got a strong technical co-founder on board. Great! The problem was, Melanie didn't know any technical people like that.

So those two weeks in San Francisco turned into three months (the full duration of her visa) as she hustled to try to find a technical co-founder. She attended every single engineering conference, reached out to people on LinkedIn, and cold-called. She had set up her 'office' in a shopping centre and was working hard from there to make it happen. She took every meeting she could.

As you can see, she was incredibly driven and conscientious. In fact, she'd often stay up late or not sleep at all just to submit documents when she'd said she would, even if those dates were completely arbitrary.

Melanie was actually an introvert, but was putting herself out there, stretching beyond her comfort zone, all to achieve what she envisioned. In fact, she even learned to kite surf when she found out that Bill Tai loved it and was hosting a startup kite surfing event, where loads of high-profile investors would be. She hated kite surfing, but did it anyway just to increase her chances of being invited.

Can you see the grit and determination? Can you see the hustle?

Melanie was still accosting software engineers everywhere she'd go, to see if they'd be interested in joining as technical co-founder. She was getting constant rejections. She was also getting constant rejections from investors (as Bill Tai's investment alone wasn't enough), even after they finally got a technical co-founder after a full year of hustling.

She attributes this to the fact that investors look for patterns, as we described in the Status chapter. As she wrote in a blog post:

... it was widely known that investors look for 'patterns' of successful entrepreneurs – Mark Zuckerberg's success meant that most were looking for a replica. We didn't tick *any* of the boxes that investors were looking for.

She recounted reading an article that described how any deviation from these desired patterns – Stanford, Harvard, MIT education, ex-Google, Apple, Facebook employee, even down to the up-and-to-the-right graphs – resulted in a negative mark. As she said, 'it would appear that we got a lot of marks, albeit negative ones. We didn't come from the "pedigree" of universities or companies and we didn't have pretty looking graphs'.

Even their Location was a potential mark against them. Virtually all the investors insisted they move to Silicon Valley, but they wanted to stay in Australia.

Melanie might not have had all the Education and Location advantages, but she did have a ton of Insight, a very clear ambitious vision, and the grit and determination to make it happen.

Yet even after building out the product that became Canva, and having fast, international growth, they still struggled to raise funding. They revised their pitchdeck over 100 times, and kept improving their pitch, bit by bit.

Eventually, they successfully landed 3 million dollars' worth of investment, half from investors in California and the other half from match funding by the Australian government grant (after having worked really hard on the application). They moved to Sydney and launched Canva in 2014. It grew like crazy, and actually became a unicorn startup (worth over $1 billion)!

Canva is an amazing story of female tech startup founder success, with an amazing product.

This is what we mean when we say success is both hard work *and* luck. Melanie's unfair advantages were her comfortable middle-class upbringing, supportive family, very high intelligence, luck, and the education and expertise she developed by jumping in at the deep end and launching her lifestyle startup (the yearbook – Fusion Books) so young. From there she started tackling her hyper-growth startup idea – which became Canva. If we had to isolate one of her unfair advantages as key, it would be her Insight. By teaching design at university, she figured out early on the problem with existing design software.

In her story you see the right personality traits and vision leading to astounding success.

Conclusion

Phew, what a journey we've just been on together.

Congratulations for getting this far.

We started this book with a reminder that life isn't fair, that luck and the randomness of life has distributed opportunity unequally. We showed how this goes a long way in explaining the statistical outliers of incredible success that we hear about in the media, and idolise in our society as role models. However, we also discussed the duality of believing in *both* luck and hard work, and using each of these mindsets as tools. This means that there is a lot to learn from the crazy success stories and self-made billionaires, but that we shouldn't compare ourselves to them as our dispositions, strengths and circumstances are all different and unique.

We discussed the luck mindset which reminds us to be grateful for what we have, and to gain a sense of contentment and acceptance with what we have in life, rather than a sense of disempowering victimhood. This mindset allows us to be compassionate, giving, kind and generous with others who may be down on their luck.

And we discussed the hard work mindset – the belief that we have the power to change the course of our lives for the better by setting goals and putting in the effort and the hours to get there. This mindset helps us dream of a better future, and then realise those dreams. It means to have a vision, to want to make your dent in the world, to want to live the life you dream of living.

We've looked at how to reconcile these two opposing mindsets by understanding the role of your own unfair advantages, to leverage your strengths and circumstances to build the future that you want, whether or not you decide to build your own startup – because the truth is, unfair advantages apply to every facet of life.

You've understood how to audit your own unfair advantages by using the MILES Framework as a lens through which to look at the many success stories you've read about. You've learned about the right mindset factors to have as a foundation. You've learned how the fixed mindset is about believing in luck, and the growth mindset is about believing in hard work. You've learned about how the truth is in the middle, with a reality-growth mindset that keeps you sane and stops you from being too hard on yourself for not becoming the next Evan Spiegel or Melanie Perkins. A mindset that keeps your mental health in check, yet one that still empowers you to push outside your comfort zone and go for it.

You've learned about how the five pillars of the Miles Framework – Money, Intelligence & Insight, Location & Luck, Education & Expertise, and Status (including your network) – all play massive roles in increasing or decreasing your chances of success, but that they also work as double-edged swords, whereby sometimes you can transform your apparent weakness into a strength with the right mindset, and by choosing the right type of startup, and the right idea to launch.

You've learned about how your 'why's are so important, both the ones related to your 'lower self' (wanting to live a certain lifestyle, increase your status and recognition, etc.)

and to your 'higher self' (wanting to have a positive impact on society or the planet). From there, you've decided what type of startup you want to start, based on your unfair advantages.

Finally, we've given you a quick primer on how to get started, and explained how funding should not be your primary aim, but rather running a real business that creates value and is sustainable (profitable, or at least eventually profitable).

This is the true power of unfair advantages – when you identify them and act upon them, your startup breaks ground. Your plans hit home with customers because you quickly get the feedback you need to adapt. Your spinning wheels find the traction they need.

And an average life turns into an extraordinary one.

People often ask us about our unfair advantages. Here they are:

Ash: I didn't have higher Education, so I didn't feel entitled and instead taught myself by reading and building an Expertise. I didn't have Money either, so I went all in and had nothing to lose. It taught me to be more creative. In terms of Intelligence, I didn't have 'book smarts' but I had 'street smarts' and good social, emotional and creative intelligence. I didn't have the best Location, but luckily I moved to London. I didn't have Status, but I built it up using my Expertise and my Inner Status with the stories I told myself.

Hasan: I didn't have much Money, but I had enough to invest in building my Expertise by taking an online business course which started me on my entrepreneurial journey. I had Intelligence in terms of 'book smarts' and was fortunate to have Location, thanks to the move from Baghdad to London when I was very young. And I happened to be in the right place at the right time to meet Ash. I didn't have Status, but I built my network proactively, and also found great mentors to learn from on my journey.

What about you? What are *your* Unfair Advantages?

Now is the time to get started.

Now is the time to take action.

Most people never get started. Be one of the few who actually do.

Find a problem to solve, speak to potential customers and users, and develop a solution based on their needs. And make sure to charge for it, otherwise it's a hobby, not a business.

This is your time to shine.

Finally, don't forget about the importance of gratitude. Whenever you feel thoughts spiralling, or the emotion of being hard-done-by or being wronged deep in the pit of your stomach, or you feel inadequate or like an imposter, just remember to breathe, and think about all the things in your life that you're grateful for. You'll be surprised at how many you'll find.

Let us know how you get on, and if you have any questions please do not hesitate to get in touch with us. Keep us updated on how you get on.